From **Grunt** *to* **GREATNESS!**

Phyllis –

Thank you for your commitment to greatness!

12/05

What others are saying about *From Grunt To Greatness!*

As someone who has dedicated her life to helping people live their dreams, I can say with confidence . . . READ THIS BOOK! When you follow Michael's guidance, you will experience the level of success that you dream about!
— Marcia Wieder, President www.dreamcoach.com
Author, *Making Your Dream Come True*

What a powerful book! Michael masterfully balances a self-deprecating humorous style with the confidence to challenge readers to grow and achieve their dreams. Read this book and enjoy your journey to happiness and fulfillment!
— Sandy Vilas, MCC, CEO, CoachInc.com

From Grunt to Greatness *is a perfect blend of inspiration, humor, and thought-provoking questions. If you long to think new thoughts and open new doors for living life to its fullest, this is the book for you!*
— Glenna Salsbury, Professional Speaker
Author, *The Art of the Fresh Start*

I cannot wait for others to read this book. It's great—really, really great! Michael, your honesty, humility, sense of humor, and love for others all show through, and your readers will feel these qualities, too!
— Barbara Nichols Mencer,
President Rainmaker Strategies

From Grunt to GREATNESS!

A *different* kind of self-help book . . .

By
Michael
Charest

Illustrations by
Debra Egli Brown

FROM GRUNT TO GREATNESS. Copyright © 2005 by Michael Charest. Published by Business Growth Solutions, LLC. All rights reserved. Printed in the United States of America. No part of this book may be used or reproduced in any manner whatsoever without written permission except in the case of brief quotations embodied in critical articles and reviews. For additional information contact: judy@fromgrunttogreatness.com

ISBN 0-9771570-3-2

Library of Congress Control Number: 2005906360

First Printing: October 2005
Publication Date: April 2006

Cover design by Karen Saunders, MacGraphics Services
Cover and interior illustrations by Debra Egli Brown
Edited by Barbara McNichol, Barbara McNichol Editorial

Thank You, Reader

Ever since I can remember, I have devoured self-help books and dreamed about writing my own someday. Thank you sincerely for helping make my dream a reality. I am honored to serve you on your journey from grunt to greatness.

Michael Charest
October 2005

Thank You Everybody Else!

I sincerely want to thank everyone who has graced my life. Twenty pages of this book could be dedicated to the *hundreds* of people who have contributed to my growth and development. Please know that while you may not be listed here by name, I love and appreciate you very, very much.

Thank you, Mom, for your tremendous editorial and administrative efforts, but most of all for believing in me and pushing me to get this done. To the rest of my family . . . to my Dad for teaching me the most valuable lesson in this book: "This is it!" To my sister-in-law and assistant, Julie for your tireless dedication to the company and keeping things afloat while I snuck away to coffee shops for countless hours to write. To my brother, Mark for your support of me, and for simply being the perfect brother and friend. Thank you to Katie and Nicole, my awesome nieces for being so loving and cute and reminding me that there are things in life besides work.

To my friend and illustrator Debbie Egli Brown. You have taken my idea of Griffin beyond my imagination. Thank you for bringing him to life. You are phenomenal.

To my publishing team . . . editor, Barbara McNichol and graphic designer Karen Saunders, thank you for your support in making the dream of my book become a reality.

To my *Business Growth Solutions* Executive Committee: Dawn Falbe, Denise Hedges, Barbara Nichols Mencer, and Eileen Redden. Thank you for stepping up and taking our great company to new levels while I completed the book.

To all *BGS* licensees, especially our "Founding Family" of the four mentioned above plus Rhonda Coles, April Goyer, Kathy Hagenbuch, Joan Peterkin, Karen Rothstein, Deborah Taylor, and Windy Warner. Thank you for your faith and confidence to invest in a license before it was proven. Your leadership has guided others to grow their businesses and grow their lives.

To Michelle Schubnel, president of Coach & Grow Rich. Michelle, you will always be my 'business partner' and friend.

To every client I have ever coached . . . thank you dearly for your trust. I would not be here today without each one of you. I love and appreciate you very much.

To my first coach, Leah Grant. Thank you for getting me started in this great profession. Thank you, Tom Henschel, for all the wonderful breakfast meetings teaching me about coaching. To my long-term coach, Dr. Tim Ursiny. Thank you for showing me that a loving, caring person can also be a great businessman. To my current coach, Jason Nazar. What can I say, man . . . You Rock! Hundreds of people are more successful and happy due to your phenomenal coaching.

To Sandy Vilas, president of Coach U, and past COO/VP Pam Richarde. I will never forget that my coaching journey began meeting with you after your terrific presentation in San Diego in 1998.

Thank you, Somers White, for speaking at ASU and igniting my passion to speak and motivate others. And to the International Coach Federation, especially chapter presidents around the world. Thank you so much for granting me the opportunity to blossom as a speaker.

To Thomas Leonard, founder of Coach U and Coachville. I know you are in heaven rejoicing in the success of all your mentees. I will never forget my yearlong journey with you, spreading the word of coaching during the Millennium Tour in 2000. And thank you Shirley Anderson for getting me through the tour with my sanity!

To my closest friends, Jay Frasco, Debbie Tieman, Ann Phillips, Lisa Green, Carlos and Nikki Hernandez, Ken Guerra, Jude Aoun, Kevitt Sale, Mahesh Shetty, Rick Wright, Kristin Fontana, Ed Borgatti, and Dan Sheehan.

Thank you for helping me balance work with play and for constantly asking, "How's the book coming?"

To mentors Bob Yeoman, Dave Pillsbury, Joe Guerra, John Blalock, and others. Thank you for being charismatic, passionate, and caring business leaders. I have always admired you and hope that some of your style has rubbed off on me.

To my idols in the self-help business: Oprah Winfrey, Tony Robbins, Dr. Phil, Og Mandino, Napoleon Hill, Deepak Chopra, Paolo Coehlo, Jack Canfield, Glenna Salsbury, Marcia Weider, Susan Jeffers, and the list goes on. Thank you for leading the way and inspiring me always.

To my personal trainer, Pam Sisco. Thank you for finally whipping my body into shape! In addition, thank you Matt Armstrong for your phenomenal marathon training.

And last, but certainly not least, to my best friend David Birdsall. Dave, more than any single person, you have challenged me to grow from grunt to greatness. Thank you.

Table Of Contents

1. Get Started 13
   Put Your Shirt Back On!
   Defining "Grunt" and "Greatness"
   The Paradox of "From" and "To"
   Meet Griffin
   How To Benefit From This Book

2. Wake Up! 29
   Hitting the Open Waters
   Boiling Like Frogs
   It Ain't Gonna Happen to Me!
   Ignorance Is Not Bliss
   When Your Belly Gets in the Way
   Slip Slidin' Away

3. Commit To Greatness 41
   A Bad Night's Sleep
   Make A Decision
   Time Flies Like the Wind . . .
   . . . And Fruit Flies Like Bananas!

4. Get Clear On Your Dreams 51
   Conceive-Believe-Achieve
   Pay Attention!
   A Flood of Help
   Are You Wasting 55 Percent of Your Life?

5 Build Your Belief 61
   Greatness Is Guaranteed
   Find the Proof in Algebra
   You are the Greatest Miracle in the World

6 Your Are What You Think 67
   Best in Show
   Are You a Hideous Beast?
   Wake Up Right
   Wedges and Spirals Determine Your Destiny
   Which Came First, the Chicken or the Egg?
   The Back Nine on Sunday
   PEWATO, My Ass!

7 Overcome Fear 83
   What If I Get On Oprah?
   Dirty Little Secrets
   When Great People Do Gruntish Things
      The Other Half of the Story…

8 Take Plaction! 97
   A Simple Plan
   Think it. Plan it. Do it.
   Cranking and Grinding
   Break Free From Your Bondage
   White Teeth Take Time
   Patience Soup

9 Get Coached 109

10 Expect To Be Challenged 113
   Dried Apples and McDonald's
   I'm Not Lance Armstrong
   Manage Expectations

11 Don't Give Up (Maybe) 125
   When Quitting is the Answer
   The Secret
   Frogs Really DO Pay Off!

12 Enjoy the Journey 133
   Old Milwaukee Said It Best!
   Presidents' Day
   This Is It
   "You Look Awful"
   Oh, So Close to Enlightenment

13 Celebrate Life 143
   Written in Stone
   Happy Birthday!

From Grunt to Greatness Services 147

About Michael 149

1

Get Started

Put Your Shirt Back On!

So, there I was on mile three of a ten-mile run—a marathon-training run to be exact. After *thinking about* running a marathon for the past five years, I finally committed to *doing it*.

At noon on a Tuesday in May, I was "squeezing in" a run between my appointments. On this 80-degree day running on the streets of Hermosa Beach in L.A., I was sweating like crazy but feeling unbelievably energized. I thought, "For a health grunt, I'm sure raising my game to greatness! I think I'll kill two birds with one stone. I'll take off my shirt and get a tan."

But another voice said, *"Do I really want to take off my shirt? I mean, I'm definitely dropping the pounds but I'm sure not there yet. Here I am, surrounded by all these beautiful people with six-pack abs, bronzed bodies, and perfect smiles. And they're running, rollerblading, playing volleyball, surfing, and sunning. Geez, doesn't anybody work around here? Maybe I'll keep my shirt on after all."*

From *Grunt* to GREATNESS!

My affirming voice cut in. "No, darn it. I want a tan and I'm hot! So what if I don't look like them. Who cares? I am running ten miles. I am a successful businessman and a coach. People really like me. I love myself, and I deserve to have my shirt off and get a tan if I want to!"

"Don't be ridiculous, Mike. Maybe in a few more weeks. For sure when you're down another ten pounds."

"For crying out loud, Mike . . . take off the damn shirt. Do you realize how long you've been dreaming of the day when you would feel comfortable in public without a shirt?"

Off came the shirt.

Chapter 1 — Get Started

My thoughts kept racing. I affirmed, "I made the decision and good for me. I'm going to get a nice tan."

Mile six. *"How can I possibly think I'm a stud? There sure are lots of people around. I wonder what my love handles look like from the back."*

Mile eight. "ROCK ON, Mike! You have never run this far before. YES! And you are bronzing!"

"My shirt looks like a damn skirt the way it's tucked into my shorts. Maybe I should just carry it."

"Geez, Mike, who cares? And nobody's watching you anyway. They're too focused on themselves."

I was running with a headset on, cranking Green Day to get myself fired up. Yes, I was in the zone: focused, controlled, concentrated on my breathing, pace, and water intake.

Suddenly I felt the presence of a car right next to me moving at my pace. It was so close, I could have reached out and touched it.

"How long has it been there?"

Still running with my shirt tucked into the back of my shorts, I whipped off my headset and glanced into the car. There were four of them . . . all teenagers. The kid in the front passenger seat—his arm resting on the open window, wise guy smirk on his face—leaned out the window and yelled,

"HEY, DUDE! PUT YOUR SHIRT BACK ON!"

As these hecklers sped away laughing, I was utterly and completely blown away. My thoughts raced faster than ever. "Think positive, Mike. They're just kids. They say that to everybody. Keep your shirt off. You are the man."

"Ah jeez, you shouldn't have taken the damn thing off in the first place. You want a tan? Get it in a booth! Or go run where nobody can see you. I gotta get out of L.A. I'm sick of it here, and I'm still fat."

"No, Mike . . . you're making it happen. You're training for a marathon, which is a metaphor for greatness. You're on the path. You're growing from grunt to greatness. So here's my new mantra: **My body has improved and I want it better. I'm working on it and I love myself right now.**"

∼

Can you relate to the self-talk in this story? I bet you can, for you have both grunt *and* greatness within you. I challenge you to love yourself as you pursue your potential in every area of your life. Don't ever postpone self-love for your arrival at the end of the run.

Chapter 1 — Get Started

Defining "Grunt" and "Greatness"

Let me be clear. The term "grunt" in this book has nothing to do with the military or being the "low man on the totem pole" who runs errands for the boss.

Being a grunt is three things.

First, **it's a state of mind.** It represents the negative thoughts and feelings *we all struggle with* to varying degrees, no matter what we've accomplished in life. These thoughts include insecurity, fear, mediocrity, doubt, guilt, and shame.

Second, **it means settling for less than what we are capable of.** It's when we don't strive for our goals and dreams because of our negative thoughts and feelings.

Third, **it's *the physical manifestation* of our negative thoughts and feelings**. It's not being as happy and at peace as we can and want to be. It's settling for jobs we can't stand, not having as much money as we'd like, or not being the kind of parents we want to be. In general, we aren't able to experience the kind of life we want and can achieve.

While coaching thousands of clients over the years, I have learned that it is common to have the negative thoughts, feelings, and actions of a grunt. *Most of us want more out of life than we have.*

From *Grunt* to GREATNESS!

If that describes you, know that you're *not alone!* In fact, you keep good company since almost every single person in the world—even those who appear successful—is part grunt.

I want to emphasize this: **Everybody** **struggles with** **much** **of what you struggle with.** And **many people** **struggle with** **everything** **that you struggle with.**

Read that paragraph again, because your frustration might stem from believing you're the only one who struggles with "grunt" traits. Letting go of this debilitating notion will put you on the path to greatness.

How do you define greatness?

Have you ever taken time to think deeply about how you *define* success and then how you *achieve* it?

Research shows that most people spend more time creating their grocery lists than thinking about what they want out of their lives.

During my seven years as a personal development coach, I have asked hundreds of people to articulate what success, or greatness, means to them. The list below represents a compilation of answers from the overwhelming majority:

- Happiness
- Financial freedom

Chapter 1 — Get Started

- Being in love
- Happy, healthy, and rich
- Peacefulness
- Living God's will

Isn't it interesting that not one person expressed the definition of success by including ALL of these elements? Because we don't focus on all of these areas, we sell ourselves short before we ever embark on our pursuit of greatness.

I believe the following definition beautifully captures the concept of greatness and all its dimensions. After reviewing my definition, please think deeply about how *you* define greatness.

Greatness: To enjoy peace of mind and happiness by loving yourself now, and pursuing balanced personal potential in each area of your life.

Each facet of this definition is critically important. Removing any one of these elements would render greatness flat and incomplete. Let me explain these elements further.

Peace of Mind and Happiness

When we really get down to it, most of us want *to be at peace with ourselves* and *to be happy*. Is there really anything else?

Sure, we might want a great career, more money, a wonderful love life, optimal health, and more. But isn't our desire for these things based on believing they will make us happier? And don't you know people who have these things, yet are discontented and unhappy? Sure you do! Would you consider these people successful? I bet not. Yet having "only" peace of mind and happiness is not enough, as the additional elements of our definition suggest.

Loving Yourself Now

Self-love (accepting yourself as you are now) is a critical dimension to this definition of greatness. It also ties to peace and happiness.

Can you be fully happy if you don't love yourself? I believe self-love is partly derived from being able to laugh at yourself in spite of your flaws (and this book is designed to help you do that). And, let me be blunt. **If you do not have the courage to pursue your personal potential, you will never fully love and respect yourself.**

Pursuing

Notice this element of the definition of greatness doesn't say "achieving" or "attaining." It implies that you will experience inner peace, happiness, and self-love when you *dedicate yourself to pursuing* a worthwhile goal, not only when you achieve it.

Chapter 1 — Get Started

This book is about telling the truth, so here it is: *You may not always achieve the level of greatness you desire.* Instead, consider measuring your greatness by *who you become* while pursuing your dreams.

Balance

Is a multimillionaire with a broken marriage successful? How about a CEO who never sees his/her kids? A world-renowned painter who suffers from emphysema from smoking? While these folks may enjoy greatness in a particular area, they haven't properly balanced and integrated their greatness. Therefore, they aren't as successful as they *could be*.

Please realize that full balance may never be achieved, but it's the *focus* on balance that helps you enjoy a well-rounded life and allows you to pursue true greatness.

Personal Potential

People don't truly achieve greatness until they reach their *potential* in each area of life. Notice this doesn't say "achieve what they want" in each area; it says "reach their potential."

It is your responsibility as a child of God to fully realize the potential He has given you. You have more greatness within you than you have currently manifested, guaranteed. I challenge you to continue to expand your greatness, tapping into your capacity to achieve your personal potential in each area of your life.

From *Grunt* to GREATNESS!

Your *dedication* to the balanced pursuit of greatness will make you feel alive, at peace, and happy.

Each Area of Your Life

Our lives, of course, are unbelievably complex, consisting of many facets and dimensions. For the purpose of this book, I have chosen to break our lives down into seven main areas, each representing a "panel" of the **Umbrella of Life.**

The panels are listed below. Please note that in Chapter 3, you will be encouraged to define what greatness means *to you* in each area. It is important that **you** do this, not me. For clarity, however, I have included a brief overview of what each panel might cover for you.

- Family—Relationships with parents and other family members, being a great mother or father

- Love—Finding a soul-mate, being in love, being the best partner you can be

- Career—Creating a thriving business, being happy at work, being a model employee or manager

- Mindset—Thinking positive thoughts, being grateful, loving yourself, being at peace, connecting with God

- Health—Enjoying optimal health and energy, being physically fit, being happy with your body

Chapter 1 — Get Started

- Finances—Being debt free, achieving financial freedom, having a savings and retirement plan
- Fun- Enjoying social time with friends and family, pursuing hobbies and passions outside of work

Consistent with the "balance" portion of our definition of greatness, I challenge you to pursue your personal potential in *every one* of these areas.

The Umbrella of Life

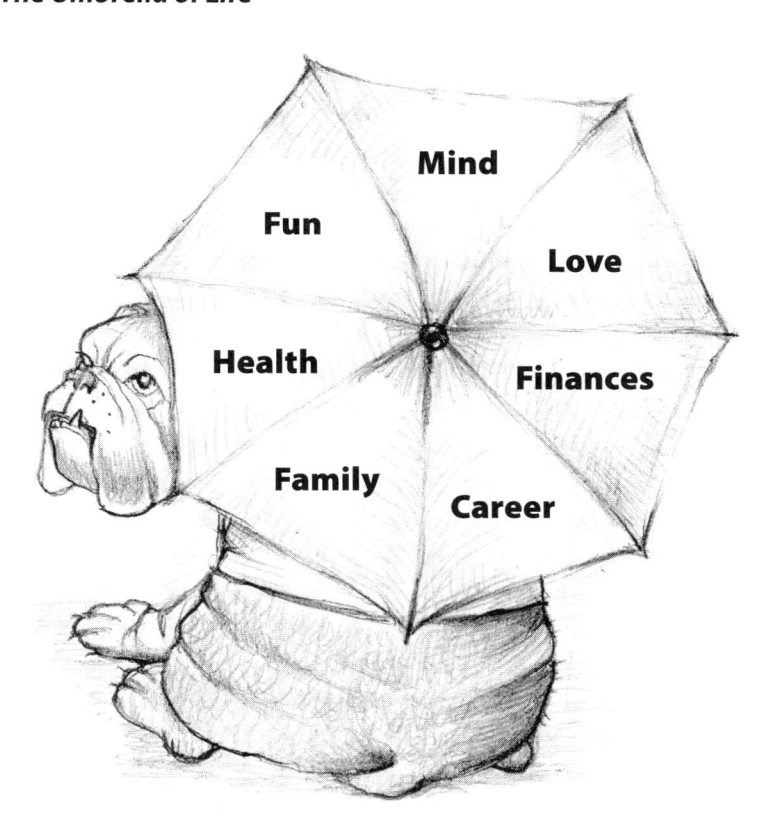

The Paradox of "From" and "To"

You may assume the purpose of this book is to help you evolve *from* grunt *to* greatness. Yes, that's true; I absolutely challenge you to shed your gruntness and reach for your personal level of greatness.

However, the from/to wording is a bit misleading. The most powerful way to evolve *from* grunt *to* greatness is to accept and love yourself *as you are*. Because the principle "that which we resist, persists" is at play here, I suggest you don't resist your gruntness but *embrace* it. This does not mean, however, that you should settle for less. Instead, I encourage you to go easy on yourself. While you may stop being a grunt in one area, you may always struggle with grunt characteristics in other areas. Accept this fact and fully love yourself anyway. This book shows you how.

Meet Griffin

I love hanging out in coffee shops. On a beautiful summer morning, I was in my favorite—the eclectic Novel Café in Venice Beach, California. I was focused on this book, thinking deeply about the *From Grunt to Greatness* title, its brand and image. Specifically, I was searching for a symbol or a character that represented the duality of our struggle concerning both gruntness and greatness.

Sitting at my favorite table in a corner with a floor-to-ceiling window view, I was sketching "grunt" and "greatness" figures when I looked outside and saw a guy walking his

Chapter 1 — Get Started

bulldog. My body instantly broke out in chills. In one second, I knew this English bulldog would be my symbol.

At first glance, a bulldog might be considered an ugly dog. He is a crumpled-faced, chubby, heavy-breathing, snorting, snoring, lumbering, sleeper of a dog. Each of these characteristics spells disaster, but when you put them all together, somehow they make up a proud, strong, happy, and beautiful animal.

Do you know what the English bulldog's traits are? Pride, confidence, tenacity, steadfastness, persistence, and acceptance—traits that perfectly match a human's journey from grunt to greatness.

His Name Is No Accident

I took great care in naming our ambassador Griffin, which literally means "body of a lion, head and wings of an eagle."

Griffin, or Griff for short, personifies the need to incorporate balance in our lives. Symbolically, he blends the bulldog's lion-like traits of strength, power, charisma, and ferocity with its eagle-like traits of vision, loftiness, and the ability to soar.

What is Griffin's symbolic message to you? To pursue lofty goals and dreams with strength and confidence while you love and laugh at yourself just as you are!

How to Benefit From This Book

From Grunt to Greatness, while seemingly lighthearted at first glance, was actually carefully thought out to serve you in the most effective ways possible.

Laugh and Love Yourself

Most self help authors do not feel justified in writing their books until they have achieved the pinnacle of success. While understandable, this is not the case here! Yes, I have achieved a certain level of success in my own life, but not at the expense of losing touch with my inner gruntness. The humorous stories in this book are meant to poke fun at myself in order to encourage you to do the same… To love and laugh at yourself, not in spite of your gruntness, but because of it!

Chapter 1 — Get Started

Stories for YOU

Please note that while the fun and humorous stories *happened* to me, they are not *about* me. They are for and about *YOU*. I hope that you will read them and think, "Wow, that sounds like me. I thought I was the only one that felt like that!" It is important for you to know that you are not alone. After reading a story, recall a similar event in your life and reflect upon what it means to you in your journey to greatness.

Use Griffin

Visuals, like stories, are great teachers and are often what we most remember. Sure, Griffin is here to provide some comic relief. But moreover, he was created to anchor you to the stories and principles. If you take a moment to think about what Griffin is going through and translate this to your own experiences, you will remember the lessons long after finishing the book.

Allow Your Subconscious Mind To Work Its Magic!

Take your time. Think about the steps to greatness. Reflect on how the stories relate to you. Ponder the tough questions. If you really take the time to do this, your subconscious goes to work and **"magically," you will begin to think and act in a manner consistent with achieving your most cherished goals and dreams.**

Join me on the path to greatness . . .

From *Grunt* to GREATNESS!

2

Wake up!

> *"Six months ago I thought I was invincible. Now I don't know. Life is not working out the way I had planned."*
>
> — Dr. Peter Benton of TV show "ER"

How about you? Is your life working out the way you had planned?

Hitting the Open Waters

Sailing San Francisco Bay on my best friend, Dave's, new 50-foot yacht on a crisp October day was magical in all respects. We were off the coast of one of the most beautiful cities in the world. The bright blue, cloudless sky had none of the area's well-known perennial fog that day. It was about 72 degrees with a stiff breeze—perfect conditions for sailing.

From *Grunt* to GREATNESS!

Three of us—Dave, his brother-in-law, and me—cruised around the Bay, by the new ballpark, past Alcatraz, and under the Golden Gate Bridge. We listened to great jazz, ate gourmet food, and even had a few drinks ready to imbibe. We were on our way to Half Moon Bay to spend the night and head back the next day—a perfect "guy weekend" and an ideal sail.

That is, until we hit the open ocean beyond the Golden Gate Bridge.

In my wildest dreams, I couldn't have guessed how quickly the water could change between the Bay and the open ocean. Within moments, 25 knot winds and a five foot swell tossed the boat around. I made the mistake of going below deck to the head. In a matter of seconds, I was heaved three times from one side of the galley to the other. I had absolutely zero control of my movements and no ability to brace myself. My head smashed into the wall and started bleeding. I nearly blacked out. A few minutes

Chapter 2 — Wake Up!

later, I threw up for the first of four times in the next four hours. From sailing high, I sunk to utter misery in a matter of minutes!

Are you throwing up over the edge of life?

This question describes how many of us go through life. We feel like we've been tossed to and fro, up and down, and side to side, with little or no control or sense of direction. We lack a sense of intent and purpose. All too often, we allow the circumstances of day-to-day activity—life's high winds—to dictate our direction.

Our sailing trip had a surprise in store for us on the next day's return as well. As we crossed back under the Golden Gate Bridge, we found a body floating in the water. Until that moment, I had only seen one dead person in my life—in a funeral parlor after she'd been prepared for viewing. That was difficult enough, but after two days in the water, this guy didn't even look human. In fact, until we decided to call the Coast Guard, I thought a dummy was floating in the water as part of a sick joke. When the Coast Guard arrived, one of them yelled to another, "It must be the jumper from yesterday."

As he was floating, we could see this guy was clothed in a pair of khakis and a nice shirt. I thought about him and his life, about the family he'd probably left behind. What in his life could have been so bad that he would end it by jumping off the Golden Gate Bridge? I felt deep sadness for him.

Do you sometimes feel like jumping off a bridge?

The first step in growing from grunt to greatness is to wake the hell up! Quit wandering aimlessly. Starting right now, ask, "Am I living on purpose? Am I seizing control of my destiny? Am I on track to achieve my goals and dreams? Or am I out of control and throwing up over the edge of life?"

Boiling Like Frogs

Yes, it seems like a gross concept, but I heard about this anecdote years ago and it has never left me, so I feel compelled to share it with you.

Now, I have not tried this myself, but I understand that if you put a frog in a pot of hot water, it will jump out immediately. However, if you put a frog in a pot of tepid water and *slowly* turn up the heat, the frog will remain in the pot until it eventually boils to death.

Chapter 2 — Wake Up!

Why does this happen? As you might guess, when the heat gets turned up slowly, the frog doesn't perceive the temperature increase and its body adjusts to the changes until it can adjust no longer.

Are you boiling to death incrementally?

Please turn back and re-read the telling quotation at the beginning of this chapter. Is it possible you have slowly and imperceptibly gotten so far off path in reaching your goals that you don't even realize you're slowly boiling to death?

If you're a parent, think back and remember when you first became a mom or dad. What kind of parent did you envision being? Did you picture yourself doing homework with your sons or daughters in a patient, thoughtful way? Did you think you would have a meal with them each day and discuss their futures? Did you envision a "special outing" with your child once or twice a month? Did you want to coach his/her little league team? *Are you doing these things or are you off the path and slowly boiling like a frog?*

When you took the new job, what kind of manager did you promise yourself you'd be? The kind of manager/leader that you always wish you'd been able to work for? Perhaps you envisioned conducting reward parties, taking your team to lunch once a month, and really taking the time to do comprehensive and thoughtful employee reviews. *Are you this manager or are you boiling to death like a frog?*

How about your health? Still vowing to take better care of your body? Or vowing to quit smoking next week? *Do it now . . . quit boiling like a frog!*

What about your overall goals and dreams? Did you dream of writing a book, seeing more plays, traveling, or starting your own business? *Are you doing it or boiling like a frog?*

⁓

Before you continue to read, sit quietly for a moment and reflect. Take a deep breath. Ask the questions in this chapter again . . . slowly. And pay attention to your answers. Be honest with yourself and feel the pain. It will help you commit to pursuing your personal potential.

It Ain't Gonna Happen to Me!

By now, you're likely saying, "I won't let my dreams go unfulfilled."

I can relate. It's like the commercial for an investment company I saw 15 years ago. Imagine a guy on the screen, mid-thirties, balding, with a slight paunch. He's sitting alone at his kitchen table reviewing his bills, debt, and non-existent investment portfolio. He's visibly depressed.

The caption at the end of the commercial read something like, "Someday soon you will be 40 years old. How are *you* going to feel if you are in this man's position?"

Chapter 2 — Wake Up!

I vividly remember my reaction at the time. I was 23 years old, fresh out of college, and holding a great position as a hotel manager. Skinny and a bit cocky, I viewed the world as my oyster.

As if it were yesterday, I remember thinking, "Yeah right! I'll never find myself in the position of that bozo—40 years old with debt and no investments. Hell, I'll be a millionaire by then!"

How close are you now to those dreams of a 23 year old?

Do you remember feeling this way? What big dreams did you have when you were 23? What kind of person did you imagine yourself being? What kind of money did you expect to make? How much traveling did you want to do? What kind of career did you envision having?

Ignorance Is Not Bliss

One day, I heard a great radio spot for a car dealership. The Johnsons were shopping for a new car. Their loan manager was running a credit check and announced over the dealership loudspeaker for all to hear: "Mr. Johnson, please report to the manager's office. We have a problem with your credit."

A moment later, the loan manager saw the husband curled up in a ball like a baby on the dealership floor. Again, over the loudspeaker, he asked the wife, "What's the matter with him? Should I call 911?" The wife replied, "He's okay.

He thinks when he does this, he can become invisible. He does it all the time when he doesn't want to deal with something."

I laughed out loud seeing this grown man curled up in a ball on the hard floor of a car dealership!

When have you, literally or metaphorically, curled up into a ball like a baby and ignored your gruntness?

Perhaps you're in debt, but aren't committed to do something about it once and for all. Maybe you've put on weight over the years and stopped going to the gym. Now your clothes don't fit, so you wear sweats and extra-large tee shirts. How about your job—do you love it? Or are you ignoring the fact that you're more "grunt" than "great," believing ignorance is bliss?

Have you noticed that the root of the word ignorance is "ignore?" Ignoring problems or challenges won't make them go away. Ignorance is *not* bliss. Ignorance is being a grunt.

Stop ignoring your gruntness. I challenge you to address your issues and commit to taking action in pursuit of your greatness.

When Your Belly Gets in the Way

Soaking wet, dripping with sweat, I could actually wring out my shirt like it had come out of the swimming pool. Thirty minutes into my fourth-ever yoga class, the moment

Chapter 2 — Wake Up!

I had been fretting about was here again—the dreaded "happy baby" pose.

Now, I like babies as much as the next guy, but posing like one is something else entirely. The "happy baby" pose requires you to lie on your back, bring your knees to your chest, and "hug" them with your arms. In yoga, this is a resting position where you can just take a moment to recoup, love yourself, and relax.

Relax my ass! All this pose did was remind me of my big gut. You see, I couldn't reach my knees because my stomach was in the way!

So there I lay amidst lithe, long-legged, slender, beautiful, cat-like "beginners" just like me. Yeah, right. Instead of feeling at peace, comfortable, rested, and loving, I felt like a grunt. At least I wasn't curled up in a ball like the guy in the car dealership!

From *Grunt* to GREATNESS!

Feeling frustrated, I wanted to give up, sneak out the back door, and head for Burgerville. Rather, I challenged myself to "lean in" and stay with it, as out of place as I felt. In an effort to go easy on myself and not take myself too seriously, I yelled out, "I can't reach my knees . . . my belly's in the way!"

My fellow yogi's burst into laughter—warm, caring "I know what you're going through" laughter. My stress and shame immediately dissipated.

And I'd swear that my knees got closer to my chest!

~

Growing from grunt to greatness requires you to push yourself to do new things while addressing your issues. That's the challenge.

When you shine a light on these areas and begin to address them, you uncover just how far you let things go. They were hidden to some extent when you ignored the problems. So, it's uncomfortable at first, and you may feel like you're taking a step back.

But even though it feels this way, you aren't going backward. You have a big belly whether you address it or not. You are in debt whether you pay attention to it or not. You are a mediocre mom or dad whether you know it or not. So, addressing the problem isn't taking a step back.

Chapter 2 — Wake Up!

Ignorance is *not* bliss. In fact, it plainly represents a lack of self-respect and to not take action is being a grunt.

I challenge you to address your issues. Have fun with the process. Don't regard it as the end of the world. You're simply taking your first step toward greatness.

Wake up! And endeavor to pursue your greatness.

Slip Slidin' Away

I enjoy Simon and Garfunkel and have listened to their "Concert in Central Park" album about 100 times . . . no kidding. One of my favorite songs is "Slip Slidin' Away." I especially appreciate the message that tells us not to let life slip by. Read this a few times and *really think about it* because if you get it, it could change your life.

> *These are the very words she uses to describe her life*
> *She said a good day ain't got no rain*
> *She said a bad day is when I lie in bed*
> *And I think of things that might have been.*

What dreams have you let slip slide away?

The greatest pain you could ever have is lying in bed 10, 20, or 30 years from now thinking of all the things you could have been—all the things you dreamed about and let slip-slide away. Please don't let this happen to you.

From *Grunt* to GREATNESS!

3

Commit To Greatness

> *"It starts with a decision.*
> *Dedicate and commit yourself, or get out, quit."*
> — Andre Agassi
> (when asked how he climbed back to #1 ranking
> in tennis after slipping to #141)

A Bad Night's Sleep

He awoke suddenly in the middle of the night soaked with sweat, shivering and short of breath, his heart pounding out of his chest. His girlfriend, who only seconds earlier had been sleeping peacefully next to him, jumped up to help him when she saw the sweat and ghastly expression on his white face.

In that moment they were both convinced that if he didn't change his life dramatically, he would have a heart attack before his 30th birthday.

But why the heart palpitations?

He had a terrific job as the general manager of a prestigious country club in L.A. Not a department head as people assumed due to his young age of 28, but the GM, the head honcho of a $200 million mountain property featuring 27 holes of pristine golf, 17 tennis courts, and three restaurants.

So, why the discontent?

He was combining his love for golf, business, and leadership. He headed a management team of 13 and presided over 138 employees and 1,500 members. He wore nice suits, was paid six figures, golfed with celebrities, and dined with people recognizable by first names only.

"What the hell is the matter with me?" he asked himself. "Why do I feel so unhappy?

Over time, he had to acknowledge that he'd been suppressing his true dreams. He identified an incongruence, a disconnect, or a gap, between what he was doing and what he really wanted to be doing.

Ever since he could remember, he devoured self-help books. He went to motivational seminars, bought self-improvement audio programs, and admired those who could inspire others to pursue their goals and dreams.

But he wasn't going for his! His main goal in life was to own his own personal development company, coach people to reach their goals, and speak and write for a living.

That night, lying in bed soaked with sweat and breathing heavily, *I made the decision to pursue my innermost dream.* It was time.

How about you? Do you feel a void in your life? A disconnect between the person you are and the one you want to be?

It's time to . . .

Make a Decision

The decision *you must make* will serve as the foundation on which you build your greatness.

The word decision comes from the Latin root *decidere,* which means to *cut off from.* When you make a decision, you cut off all other possibilities. When you make a decision that you will pursue your potential—strive to achieve your definition of success and greatness and live the life you've imagined once and for all—it means you cut off the possibility of *not* succeeding.

That's powerful! And that's the kind of commitment you have to make in order to succeed.

I challenge you to make two critical decisions right now:

1) Decide to be great in all areas of your life.

2) Decide to **take action** and pursue your personal best in each area.

Unfortunately, people who are "trying" to achieve their goals haven't really committed to do so. Like I did for too many years, they feel out the situation, wait to see what happens, and *hope* to achieve their goals some day. *But they fail to make a commitment.*

Don't let this happen to you. The next step to go from hoping and wishing to *enjoying* your success is to make a decision.

Are you ready to make that decision?

Achieving your potential is not easy. If you don't fully commit to doing what it takes, you won't succeed. It's that simple.

When you make and *fully connect* with your decision, you will have more focus, clarity, purpose, inspiration, and motivation. As you will learn later, obstacles arise. If it were easy to achieve greatness and live a happy, healthy, exciting life, then everyone would be doing it!

Making a clear decision reminds you why you undertook this beautiful journey and why you want to succeed in life. Then, when you connect deeply with your decision and your reasons for making it, you'll be inspired to take the action necessary to succeed.

Chapter 3 — Commit to Greatness

The rest of Andre Agassi's message from the beginning of the chapter demonstrates exactly that point:

> *It starts with a decision. Dedicate and commit yourself, or get out, quit. Then create a plan with daily goals and actions. Ask yourself at the end of the day if your actions were congruent with your goals. Yes or no? Then make adjustments, be your best, and sleep well at night.*

How are you sleeping at night?

Do you sense a stirring that you could be more? Decide right here and right now to pursue your personal greatness!

Time Flies Like the Wind . . .

In 10th grade at Agawam High School in Agawam, Massachusetts, I had Mr. Pulaski for my geometry teacher. Thankfully, "Mr. P" knew that this subject could be boring and/or difficult for those students not interested in mathematics. So he combated the inherent challenges by incorporating creativity, zest, and humor into his teaching. He tossed rubber frogs at napping students, conveyed messages through comic strips, and rewarded students with prizes.

His classroom was full of posters, pictures, comics, and clever sayings. All these years later, I still remember their messages. One posted in the middle of the large clock on the wall said, "Time is passing. Are you?" Another said, "Time flies like the wind, and fruit flies like bananas."

Get it?

~

If you're over 35 years old, I don't have to tell you how fast time goes by. If you're younger than 35, you probably don't care. But trust me; you will *soon enough!*

Yes, it's true: Greatness takes time. But in case you haven't figured it out yet, time passes whether you decide to pursue your greatness or not. Why not make progress while it does?

Chapter 3 — Commit to Greatness

In one year, you'll either be where you are now or closer to your dream. Time is relative. It may feel like time drags during the pursuit of a worthwhile goal; however, it will seem like no time passed at all when you have reached it.

You can turn your whole life around in one year. You have a choice. In one year from today, you could either be slimmer, fatter, or the same as you are now. You could either have more savings, less, or about the same as now. You could be enjoying a more loving, intimate, happier relationship with your spouse or not. You could have found the love of your life or still be single. You could have a closer connection to God or still be searching.

How do you want to look back on your time?

Right now, identify one area of your life in which you are a grunt. It could be any one of the panels in the Umbrella of Life (family, career, health, finances, love, mindset, and fun). Take a moment and dream about where your life could be one year from now in that area.

- Could you have that dream job?
- Could you be 50 pounds lighter if needed?
- Could you find your soul mate?
- Could you save $12,000 or more?
- Could you have written that book that you've always dreamed about writing?

From *Grunt* to GREATNESS!

Make a decision and commit to the path of greatness. In one year, you can look back to this very day with pride and a sense of accomplishment. Or, you can look back and chalk up another year of wasted time . . . another year of failed attempts, of mediocrity, of gruntness.

The choice is yours. One thing is for sure: The year is going to pass whether you decide to pursue greatness or not!

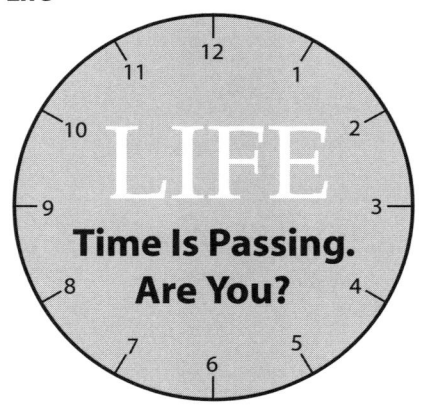

"The Clock of Life"

LIFE
Time Is Passing. Are You?

Now, lest this chapter gets too serious, here's a story about perfection to share with you. Remember, this book is not a manual on how to become a superhuman, perfect machine. It's about committing to be better, to reach for your personal potential in all areas of your life. It's also about *loving yourself now,* as your life is now—with all your flaws, imperfections, and insecurities.

Chapter 3 — Commit to Greatness

... And Fruit Flies Like Bananas!

At 5:00 a.m. one morning, I quickly jumped out of bed, excited to get some writing done at Novel Café before heading to a motivational speech I was to deliver later that afternoon.

I showered fast, answered and sent about 20 emails, packed my stuff, and raced out the door at 6:00 a.m. Dressed like I'd just stepped off the pages of *GQ* in a tailored suit, silk tie, and polished shoes, I felt confident, alive, and passionate—like a man on the path to achieving greatness.

Climbing into my new silver convertible, top down, I thought, "This car really needs to be washed." It was filthy, littered with empty water bottles, sweat towels, and food wrappers. I'd even left an apple core and banana peel, which were now decaying on the floor. I immediately felt like a grunt, but was too eager to get to the coffee shop and didn't want to clean the car at that moment.

Because it was a cool, foggy morning, I put the top up and turned the heater on. Well, once the air got moving and stirred things up, a swarm of fruit flies swirled around inside the car. There must have been 50 of them! And with the car enclosed for the first time in days, the aroma of rotten banana peel wafted through the air. It smelled disgusting.

Traveling down the road, I had been feeling on top of the world. I had my nice car, nice suit, nice tunes, and life

From *Grunt* to GREATNESS!

was good, but the picture—and my mood—completely changed because of my grunt tendencies. I was surrounded by a banana peel, an apple core, food wrappers, and a bunch of buzzing fruit flies that were annoying the hell out of me.

~

So, I ask you: That morning, was I a grunt or great? If you said grunt, give me some credit—I looked terrific, had been working since 5:00 a.m., was going to deliver a great talk, and was driving a nice car.

If you said great, did you ignore the fruit flies and the five-day-old banana peel?

If you said, both grunt and great—right on. Or as I like to say, ROCK ON! Yes, I am both and always will be in some form or another. And so will you!

Are you slipping on banana peels?

If you beat yourself up for your grunt tendencies, doing so gets you nowhere. Cut yourself some slack. Quit being a martyr. Love yourself. Realize that you are perfect now, yet you will never be perfect. Then make a decision to pursue greatness. I know it seems like a paradox, but isn't it great?

And if you're one of those who feel you have to be perfect all the time, forget it. Relax. Laugh at yourself. Eat a banana!

4

Get Clear On Your Dream

"If one advances confidently in the direction of his dreams, and endeavors to live the life he has imagined, he will meet with success unexpected in common hours."

— Henry David Thoreau

Take a big, long, powerful, deep breath. In through your nose . . . count to five as you inhale . . . out slowly through your mouth. Count to five as you exhale. Take a moment to get into a peaceful state and continue breathing deeply for a moment.

Imagine you're standing on top of a gentle, rolling, grass-covered hill. You're overlooking a lovely valley with a magnificent crystal blue lake.

It's a beautiful, sunny day—a crisp 70 degrees—and a gentle breeze complements the warm sun on your face. A few snow-white, billowy clouds float above, enhancing an azure sky.

From *Grunt* to GREATNESS!

You lie down on the hill, aware of the plush soft grass beneath you. The angle of the hill conforms perfectly to your spine. You stretch your body over its support and gaze at the sky. You feel on top of the world . . . fulfilled, at peace, content, and happy.

Imagine that you are reflecting on the state of each area of your life and relishing the fact that you have achieved incredible success in all of them.

You have achieved financial abundance. You are deeply in love. You are a terrific, patient, engaged parent. You enjoy health and wellness. You are lean with lots of energy. You have the job of your dreams. Perhaps you own your own business. You know how to have fun and engage in play regularly. You are connected deeply and lovingly to God. Your mind thinks positive, peaceful thoughts. You have friends you respect and love. Whatever it is you want in life, you have it!

Chapter 4 — Get Clear On Your Dream

Feel the moment!

How do you feel? Confident? Energized? Rich? Peaceful? Happy? What else do you feel? Just sit and enjoy the moment. Really get into it.

Conceive — Believe — Achieve!

In the self-help masterpiece, *Think And Grow Rich,* Napoleon Hill beautifully makes the case that if you can *conceive* your ideal life (think it), then you can achieve it. The very fact that you can call to mind the mental picture of what you want your life to look like, proves that you have the capacity to make it come true. Otherwise you would not have been able to imagine it in the first place!

Please read this again and think about it, because if you can agree with this concept with all your heart, it will absolutely transform your life. The very fact that you can conceive your dream life *proves* that you can achieve it!

∼

So, the next step in your path to greatness is to conceive your vision in each panel of the Umbrella of Life (Health, Career, Family, Finances, Mindset, Love, and Fun).

Take a moment now to vividly imagine what greatness would look like to you in each area. Thinking about this now will make the future steps and principles in this book more effective because you can begin to apply them to *your real life wants and desires.*

Ready to Dig Deeper?

Let's go even deeper and think about your *purpose* in life.

What were you put on this earth to do? What is your calling, your mission, your vocation? How will this planet be better because you have lived on it?

We have addressed striving for greatness within each panel of the Umbrella of Life. In addition, God has planted in you an all-encompassing grand purpose, a mission, a dream for your life. Consider it your responsibility to uncover what this mission is and fulfill it.

Many people have asked how to identify their purpose in life because they haven't yet figured it out. It is my contention that you *do* know what your purpose is, you just may be suppressing it, similar to what I had done when I managed the golf resort.

If you think deeply and reflect on the questions throughout this book, you'll uncover the desire within you. The very fact that you have this desire (as long as it is a positive desire) indicates that it is *God's will* for you, otherwise *you would not have had the thought to begin with*. He is planting the thought within your mind.

Pay Attention!

It was March 4, 2001. While attending Mass at Saint James church, I was thinking about the challenges my business was enduring.

Chapter 4 — Get Clear On Your Dream

It had been a while since I had attended church. Father McNamara was feeling bolder than usual or he had adopted a new style. He stepped down from the altar and spoke passionately from the middle aisle of the packed church to over 500 parishioners.

I was sitting along the aisle in about the 20th pew, so he had to do a bit of walking to get to my area. But there he stood right in front of me. His sermon was about praying to God and asking for His desire for our lives—to relinquish our lives to Him and live according to His plan.

Father uttered the words "Live God's dream." As he did so, he looked directly into my eyes and touched my forearm. Just as he spoke the words, and I mean at the precise moment, a ray of sunlight pierced through the ceiling window and struck me right in the face. It was so obvious that Father McNamara noticed it and winked at me.

Geez, I get goose bumps even four years later writing about this experience. *It was magical. It was divine. It was a sign.* Whatever doubts I had at the time about my mission, my calling, my vocation, or my purpose vanished at that moment.

The message to me was, "My desire for you, Michael, is to help others reach their goals and dreams, and thus, you will do the same."

From *Grunt* to GREATNESS!

What signs have you experienced?

You, too, have received such signs, I'm certain. Please commit to paying attention to signs that come your way. Once you identify your vision, open yourself up and look around for signs that validate your desire. They will come and when they do, allow them to reinforce your commitment.

A Flood of Help

Have you heard the story about a man whose neighborhood was engulfed in a massive flood? It came so quickly that he had to climb on the roof of his home to avoid being swept up in the waters. A religious man, he prayed, asking God to save him.

Moments later, his neighbor came floating down the street in a life raft. He made his way over to the man and shouted, "There's room for both of us here. Climb down and grab on."

The man yelled back, "That's okay. You go ahead, God will save me."

A half-hour later, the water had reached an ever-higher level and a boat came by. The boatman encouraged the man to climb aboard and be rescued from the flood. The man exclaimed, "Thank you, but I will be fine. God will save me."

Chapter 4 — Get Clear On Your Dream

Finally, a rescue helicopter hovered overhead. They dropped a rescue line to the man and announced over the loudspeaker, "Strap yourself in . . . You'll be fine."

Once again, the stubborn man turned down the offer.

Well, sadly enough, the water continued to rise, eventually sweeping the man and his house away. When he arrived at the Pearly Gates, he asked God, "What happened? I believed in you. I trusted that you would save me."

God, in a loving, but exasperated voice said, "Who do you think sent the life raft, boat, and helicopter?"

Sometimes when we receive signs, we have a tendency to ignore them. We think, "That was too easy, it must just be a coincidence." **There are no coincidences. These are signs from God that you are on the path to greatness.**

Are You Wasting 55 Percent of Your Life?

Do you know that on average, pre-retirement adults spend 55 percent of their lives getting ready for, driving to, thinking about, and recuperating from WORK?

In addition, statistics show that approximately 70 percent of Americans are unsatisfied in their careers. This means that seven out of every ten people in the United States alone are feeling unhappy or unfulfilled for *more than half of their waking hours!*

From *Grunt* to GREATNESS!

Years ago, it was certainly understandable to choose a job for the sole purpose of putting food on the table and a roof over your head. I doubt many people in the late 19th century had the luxury of searching for enlightenment in their work.

But with modern-day technology, the Internet, more technical schools to learn specific trades, and more accessibility and opportunities to attend college, it has never been easier to make a good living *doing exactly what you want to do,* including starting your own business.

Don't get me wrong. I'm not saying you won't face challenges. And, I don't recommend quitting your job without a well thought out plan when you have financial and familial responsibilities. I am saying, however, that you have no excuse for being miserable in your career.

Consider a passage from Dorothea Brande's book *Wake Up and Live!* This book, published in 1936 during the depression, is one of the most hard-hitting and riveting books I have ever read. The author wrote:

> In the long run, it makes little difference how cleverly others are deceived; if we are not doing what we are best equipped to do, or doing well what we have undertaken as our personal contribution to the world's work, at least by way of an earnestly followed avocation, there will be a core of unhappiness in

our lives which will be more and more difficult to ignore as the years pass.

Are you ready to be happy?

Decide now to pursue your greatness and live a happy life by fulfilling your calling in work and in each area of your life. You owe it to God and to yourself.

From *Grunt* to GREATNESS!

5

Build Your Belief

"The thing always happens that you really believe in; and the belief in a thing makes it happen."

— Frank Lloyd Wright

Greatness Is Guaranteed

We gathered by the Malaga Cove fountain in beautiful Palos Verdes. At 7:00 a.m. on a Saturday, most of us would have rather been cuddled up in bed. In fact, looking around at some of the lovely women in our group of 17, I would have rather been cuddled up in bed with any one of them!

It was foggy and cool. Because nobody knew each other, we were quiet and a bit unsure of ourselves. We were also nervous and wondering what we had gotten ourselves into.

And then he spoke . . .

From *Grunt* to GREATNESS!

"I GUARANTEE you, that if you follow this program, you will complete your first marathon six months from now, on October 12th, 2003."

"Let me repeat myself. I guarantee you will run your first marathon on October 12th if you follow the program. I know you don't believe it yet, but trust me. You will."

I was fired up. My sleepiness, desire to climb back in bed, and wandering eyes at the attractive women—all of it evaporated and coach Matt had my undivided attention. In fact, as I looked around, I noticed he'd grabbed everyone's attention.

What Coach Matt was saying made perfect sense. Preparing to run a marathon is broken down into three main areas: physical training, proper nutrition, and mental endurance. If you follow a prescribed plan to grow and perform in these three areas, you can complete a marathon.

Now that is greatness!

That morning, completing a marathon was our collective vision. Coach Matt knew the importance of nurturing belief and *allowed us to feed off his until we built our own.*

I so appreciated his belief in us and his confidence in his training system that, in an instant, *I believed for the first time in my life that I could run a marathon.*

Chapter 5 — Build Your Belief

Greatness is Guaranteed!

Let me do for you what coach Matt did for us. If you follow the prescribed plan in this book, **you will achieve greatness** *as it has been defined.* Indeed, **you would not have been granted the gift of conceiving your vision without the corresponding ability to make it come true.**

Now that you have conceived your vision, you must continually build your belief and confidence in order to achieve your greatness.

Find the Proof in Algebra

Specifically, how does belief in yourself translate to greatness? Well, the answer can be found, of all places, in an algebraic equation.

I know when you were taking algebra in school, you complained, "This is ridiculous. I'm never going to use this in everyday life." Well, now your greatness depends on it. Isn't that cool? Thank you, algebra teachers!

Under a math property called the "Substitution Property of Equality" we can say that

If A=B, and B=C, then A=C.

Remember this from your school days? Simple enough, isn't it?

From *Grunt* to GREATNESS!

Here's how it relates to greatness. As we will discuss more in Chapter 7, if you take enough action, keep moving toward attaining your goals and dreams and do not give up, you will eventually achieve them. *Action is absolutely critical to attaining greatness.*

Well, your ability to keep pushing forward and taking action is 100 percent contingent upon your belief in yourself. Look at people who boldly take action and I guarantee you they have belief, faith, and confidence in themselves and will absolutely achieve greatness. Conversely, when people don't take action, and/or they give up too soon, it is because they lack belief and, therefore, will never achieve their goals.

Thus, our *Greatness Theorem* looks like this:

> If A (Greatness) = B (Action), and
> B (Action) = C (Belief), then
> A (Greatness) = C (Belief)

If you believe in yourself and in your destiny, you will keep taking action and ultimately achieve your goals and dreams.

Know that *I BELIEVE IN YOU!*

I have coached too many people toward greatness to not believe in this "grunt to greatness" system. Please trust me and allow

Chapter 5 — Build Your Belief

my belief in you to carry you, as Coach Matt did with me and the others who used his system to prepare for a marathon.

You are the Greatest Miracle in the World

If you haven't yet done so, please read *The Greatest Miracle in the World* by Og Mandino. In this wonderful book from the man I consider to be the greatest self-help genius ever, you'll read "Memorandum from God," reminding you what a beautiful miracle you are. It affirms that you are capable of achieving levels of greatness beyond what you may currently believe. Here is an excerpt:

> With all the combinations at my command, beginning with that single sperm from your father's four hundred million, through the hundreds of genes in each of the chromosomes from your mother and father, I could have created three hundred thousand billion humans, each different from the other.
>
> But who did I call forth? You! One of a kind. Rarest of the rare. A priceless treasure, possessed of qualities in mind and speech and movement and appearance and actions as no other who has ever lived, lives, or shall live.
>
> Imitate no one. Be yourself. Show your rarity to the world and they will shower you with gold.

From *Grunt* to GREATNESS!

Do you believe you are the greatest miracle?

If you doubt that you can start your own business, become a millionaire, be a better parent, write a book, buy a dream home, lose weight, or quit smoking, c'mon. Know that you are a miracle—the greatest miracle in the world!

Embrace your gruntness and believe that you can and will achieve greatness, not *in spite of* your gruntness, but *because of it!*

Dedicate a portion of every single day for the rest of your life to building your belief in yourself.

~

For a free report on daily strategies and exercises on how to build and reinforce your belief, please visit my website at www.fromgrunttogreatness.com.

6

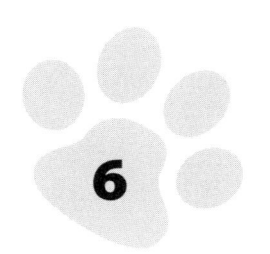

You Are What You Think

"We are what we think. All that we are arises with our thoughts. With our thoughts, we make the world."
— Buddha

Best in Show

"Come over here and sit down, you fat, drooling, dumb excuse of a dog!"

My best friend Dave's dog is a 185-pound Newfoundland named Zephyr. In 2004, a Newfoundland won the "Best in Show" award at the American Kennel Club's celebrated event at Madison Square Garden. But Zephyr is no "best in show." (Sorry, Dave.) He drools a lot, rolls around in the dirt, swims in ponds, plays in the backyard pool and is chlorine-bleached and smelly as a result.

But, of course, Dave would never talk to Zephyr that way. Zephyr is a beautiful animal. He is loving, obedient, trusting, intelligent, and endearing.

And so are you. (Well, maybe not the obedient part!)

I bet your stomach turned when you read this chapter's opening passage. You wouldn't ever speak to your dog like that . . . right? Yet I am willing to bet that *you have had similar thoughts about yourself.*

How many times have you looked in the mirror and said awful things to yourself about your chin, thighs, love handles, cellulite, wrinkles, and more?

Have you ever berated yourself for a poor shot on the golf course? Have you beaten yourself up about your relationships, your career choices, or your lack of money?

What were you thinking?

I challenge you to recall your thoughts—even just those from today. Were any of them negative? Think about what you say to yourself when you look in the mirror, assess your career, your finances, your marriage, your dating skills, and so on.

Are You a Hideous Beast?

I was watching an episode of "The Oprah Winfrey Show" on TV one day when Oprah was interviewing teenagers about their struggles growing up in today's society. One young woman, perhaps 13 years old, caught my attention in the montage of clips. She was cute and affable with an infectious smile, yet underneath she seemed to be hiding something. When it came her turn to share her thoughts

Chapter 6 — You Are What You Think

about herself, she broke down in tears and referred to herself as a "hideous beast." She went on to say that she was "disgusting," "a pig," and "a loser." She even complained that she had a "Jay Leno chin."

I was shocked to the core at the raw brutality with which she viewed herself. She was so open, authentic, and exposed. How could such a beautiful girl think those things about herself? What has happened to her that she has such low self-esteem?

But then I remembered conversations with family members, friends, and clients. I realized that many, if not all of us, partake in this type of self-criticism.

Ahhh, Jay Leno's chin, JLo's butt, Bob Hope's nose, Seal's facial scar, Gandhi's poverty, Nelson Mandela's criminal record, Bob Dole's erectile dysfunction . . .

Hideous beasts? Losers? I think not.

What is your subconscious programming?

Your subconscious mind does not know the difference between what is actually true (reality) and *what you tell it is true*. However you program your subconscious, your mind works to prove you correct. Therefore, if you tell yourself you are a loser, or fat, or poor, or a bad person, or a hideous beast, or even a lousy golfer, your subconscious triggers you to *act in a way that proves that to be true*. That's the bad news.

The good news is that when you program your subconscious via your thoughts that you are intelligent, handsome, beautiful, powerful, a terrific parent, a philanthropist, and so on, then your subconscious proves that to be true and *triggers you to act consistently with those thoughts.*

Your path to grunt or greatness is only thoughts away.

Wake Up Right

Beep. Beep. Beep. Beep. Beep.

The alarm sounds. You think to yourself . . .

"I am excited for a great day today. I am going to finish that big project at work. I'm going for a walk first. What a great way to start the day. Then I'll read some inspirational material, practice yoga, and eat healthy. I am going to get a lot accomplished."

Or not.

"Boy, this bed feels awesome. I love my comforter. It's like a womb in here. Maybe I'll just stay in bed all day. Watch videos. I've got two left over from last night. Oohh, that would be fun. I could make some popcorn, eat leftover pizza, and just make it a movie day! I wish it were raining out. That would make it even more enjoyable."

Which of these two people is more likely to have a powerful, thriving, successful day?

Chapter 6 — You Are What You Think

Remember the saying, "You are what you eat?" In addition, *you are what you think*. And the results you experience in life are in direct response to your thoughts. And there are no more important thoughts than the first few of each day.

What's the first thing you *think about* the moment you wake up? What is the first thing you *do?*

I predict that your answers determine, to a large extent, whether you're a grunt or on the path to greatness. When I ask these two questions of prospective clients, their answers tell me a whole lot about them. Here's a sampling of their answers:

- "Hit the snooze button."
- "Roll over and go back to bed."
- "Think about all the shit I gotta deal with at work."
- "Drink a glass of water and go out for a walk."
- "Get out of bed right away and begin my morning meditation."

All things being equal, which responses best coincide with traits of those on the path to greatness?

Wedges and Spirals Determine Your Destiny

Your first thought of the day sets the tone for your entire day.

I refer to the this first thought as a "wedge thought." Think of the shape of a wedge—narrow at one end and gradually widening at the other. The thought itself is so small, so seemingly miniscule, so narrow. Yet like a wedge, it creates leverage and opens up possibilities, setting the tone for activities and outcomes throughout the day.

You can begin your day with either a positive or negative wedge—it's your choice. In fact, you "wedge" your day whether you realize it or not. You can do it by default (without thought) or be proactive and positive, and begin your day with enthusiasm.

Your early-morning wedge thought, whether positive or negative, determines the direction of your spiral, or momentum, for the day. A positive wedge thought creates an upward spiral of positive things happening throughout the day. Conversely, a negative wedge thought sets into motion a negative, downward spiral. Negative events tend to build on one another. As in physics, an object in motion stays in motion until its pattern gets interrupted. So interrupt any negative pattern you've established with new, more positive thoughts.

Chapter 6 — You Are What You Think

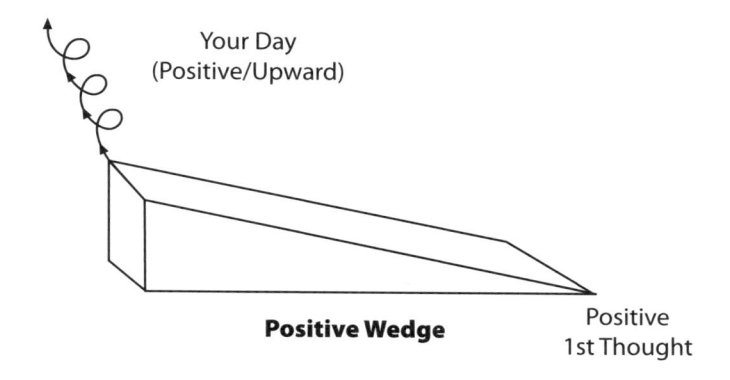

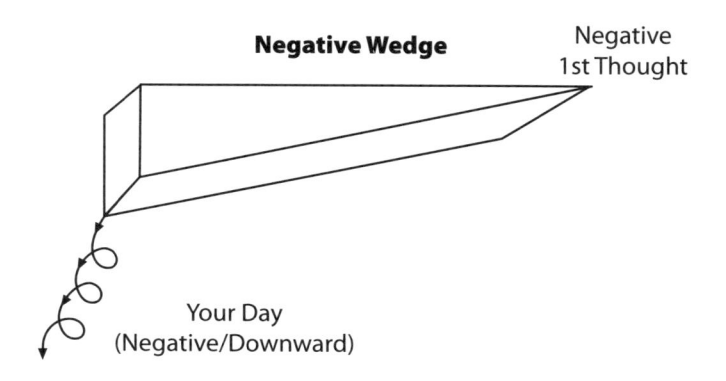

Your Day
(Positive/Upward)

Positive Wedge

Positive
1st Thought

Negative Wedge

Negative
1st Thought

Your Day
(Negative/Downward)

From *Grunt* to GREATNESS!

As your days go, so goes your life . . .

Would you agree that your life is simply a progression of days?

The graphic below further illustrates the importance of your thoughts and the impact on your *life*. As the outcome of your day is contingent upon your first thought and subsequent spiral, your entire life is similarly linked to the outcome of your days!

You are what you think.

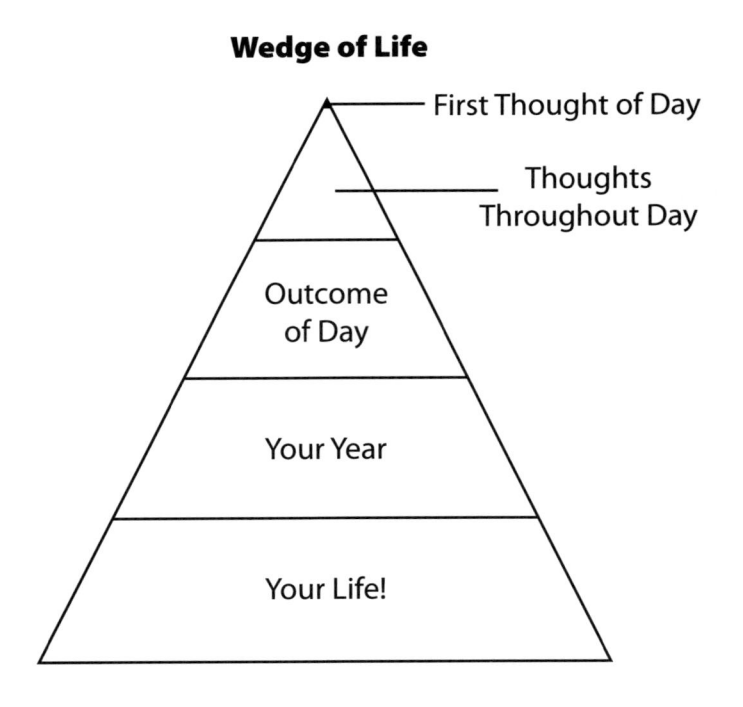

Wedge of Life

- First Thought of Day
- Thoughts Throughout Day
- Outcome of Day
- Your Year
- Your Life!

Chapter 6 — You Are What You Think

Which Came First, the Chicken or the Egg?

Do you have a tendency to believe that you'll be happy or love yourself more once you get what you want?

You may think, "Once I lose my belly, I'll stop beating myself up." Or "When my business is successful, then I'll be happy." Or "I just need to get out of debt, then everything will be all right."

However, the opposite is actually far more accurate. *You'll get what you want once you're happy and love yourself. Whether you call it the chicken or the egg, happiness and self-love precede getting what you want. Not the other way around.*

That means it is imperative to focus on and think about what you *do* want, not what you *don't* want. Remember, your subconscious brings into the physical world what you think about the most. So, if you think about being overweight, or being in debt, or being single, or hating your job, look out! Because you are flat-out in trouble and that is what you are going to get.

Even though you do not want these things, your subconscious only knows that is what you are thinking about. Therefore, it assumes you want them and will get you to act in the manner that will bring about those results. That is why you have to think *in the positive* about what you want—thoughts about what you are moving *to*, not what you are moving *from*.

Replace: *"I'm fat and need to lose weight."*
With: *"I'm excited about improving my overall health and wellness."*

Replace: *"I need to get out of debt."*
With: *"I am moving toward financial abundance."*

Replace: *"This job sucks."*
With: *"It's time to pursue my ideal career."*

Do you see how the initial thoughts in each set ask the subconscious to focus on the concepts of "overweight," "debt," and "bad job" and will reinforce that you are correct? Replacing the negative thoughts with the positive will trigger your subconscious to focus on "improving your health," "financial abundance," and "ideal career."

Then you begin to act in a way that aligns you with these conditions. You'll actually start to DO things that you didn't before, such as exercising and eating healthy, spending less money and contacting a credit counselor, and ultimately pursing your true vocation.

The Back Nine on Sunday

I love the game of golf—playing it, watching it, and analyzing it as a metaphor for life. In particular, I'm struck by how Tiger Woods rarely speaks about winning golf tournaments, but rather about putting himself "in position to win on the back nine on Sunday." Tiger often says things

Chapter 6 — You Are What You Think

like, "That's all I can hope for," and "I do my best to get in a position to win."

His wording creates a key distinction. Let me explain.

A professional golf tournament consists of four 18-hole rounds of competitive golf, scheduled from Thursday to Sunday. When Tiger Woods refers to the "back nine," he speaks about the final nine holes out of 72, or the final 1/8th of the tournament that takes place Sunday afternoon. He wants to be "in the hunt" at that point with an excellent chance of winning the tournament.

Professional athletes know better than anybody the importance of mental discipline and having the right mindset to achieve their goals. Many employ professional sports psychologists to train their minds for success. *Why should we be any different?*

Like golf, life is a mental game that requires training our minds for success. It's based on a principle called "positive expectancy without attachment to outcome" or what I've nicknamed PEWATO.

Tiger exercises PEWATO on the back nine on Sunday. He wants to win; he expects to win; he prepares to win. Indeed, Tiger tries his best to win. But he's not *attached* to winning. That means he doesn't base his overall happiness and success on the results of a particular tournament, no matter how big it is.

Tiger loves playing golf. He loves the competition. He loves being in the hunt, hitting exceptional golf shots, recovering from bad ones, and playing among the crowds. Sure he loves winning too, but he talks more about his love of *competing*—the journey, not the destination.

I implore you to adopt this philosophy in your life and your personal pursuit of greatness.

∼

Chapter 6 — You Are What You Think

Identify your goals and dreams. Believe that you will achieve them and pursue them with vigor. But don't tie your happiness to the outcome. Rather, invest in the satisfaction of pursuing your personal best! Who you become in the process is far better than any single "trophy" you will acquire.

PEWATO, My Ass!

I was feeling absolutely terrific about my decision. Sure, $3,500 wasn't a drop in the bucket. But it would be worth it. I was finally doing something other than working… making a conscious effort to put myself out there and meet dozens of beautiful, single, intelligent L.A. women!

Seven years after a short-lived marriage and amicable divorce, I was tired of being single.

While I love my new career of coaching, sitting in my home office on the phone all day isn't exactly conducive to meeting women. Because I enjoy my work, the days and weeks fly by and it's easy for me to get so focused that I sometimes forget to improve the balance in my social life. That's why I joined a high-level dating service.

Sitting across from an absolutely gorgeous company representative, I wanted to ask *her* out right then and there! I'm sure she was intentionally placed in that position as their #1 marketing tool. Within minutes, she was ringing up my credit card for $3,500.

Then the calculations began.

There were 1,400 single women in the dating service library, with an estimated 900 in my age bracket. The company promotes that for every person contacted 25 percent accept a date. Not that I'd be a match for all 900 women, but this could potentially add up to 225 dates. I immediately started to stress about how I'd fit them all in. Dating two every week would take me two years plus! On the other hand, given those statistics, I was sure to find at least one woman to date and eventually fall in love with.

So much for being unattached to the outcome.

Each day that first week, I called the center. As required, I gave them my five new requests and checked to see if any responses to my previous five requests had been received. Here's a summary of my conversations with the company representatives:

Day #1
"Hi Michael. Shawna is a no, no reason given. Becky is a no, no reason given. Susan is a no, no reason given. Kristi is a no, no reason given. Sara is a no, reason 7."

"What's reason 7?"

"No chemistry."

"Shit," I said aloud. "0 for 5. I feel like a loser. Is this normal?"

Chapter 6 — You Are What You Think

"Don't worry about it, Michael. You'll get dates. Your profile looks great and you're cute. It's a numbers game; just keep submitting requests."

Day #2
"Stephanie is a no, no reason. Donna is a no, no reason. Skyler is a no, no reason. Denise is a no, no reason, and Jen is a no, with no reason given."

Day #3
See day 2 and change the names.

Day #4
See days 2 and 3 and change the names.

Over the course of six weeks, I submitted 78 names. I received four positive responses, went on two dates, and must have checked off the wrong box on the other two, as I don't even remember picking them.

The experience became a blur.

Can you even comprehend getting rejected 74 out of 78 times? That's a 95 percent failure rate! And these weren't married women with kids or 22 year olds or other ridiculous matches. They were single, close to my age of 35 at the time, and all in the damn library to get dates—just like I was!

If these pre-qualified women were saying no to me, who would say yes? *What was the problem?*

Am I too short, too heavy? Are my teeth not straight enough? Wasn't I warm enough, friendly enough, funny enough, sexy enough? Was it my career, my interests, my hobbies, my dreams?

I'm getting nauseous just thinking about this. Hey, I didn't say PEWATO is easy!

Seriously though, we must really believe that everything happens for a reason, especially our struggles. I enthusiastically believe I will find my soul mate due to my resolve to maintain a positive level of expectancy and yet remain unattached to the outcome.

How about you?

7

Overcome Fear

"Feel the fear and do it anyway."
— Susan Jeffers

What If I Get On Oprah?

I have been feeling very uneasy. Despite working out and eating well, I'm often short of breath lately and feel my heart beating harder than usual. When my brother Mark and I were golfing and I arrived at the 16th tee box panting like a dog without water, he asked what was wrong. "You seem out of sorts, Mike. Are you stressed about something?"

It suddenly became clear. I'm scared to finish my book and it's making me ill.

In fact, I have been touting this book as "90 percent complete" for six months. Back in December, I promised my friend Debbie that she would receive the completed manuscript on Monday. She and dozens of friends have regularly asked, "How's the book coming?"

My answer is similar each time: "Almost there, just a few finishing touches." I have been "finishing touching" this damn book for six months now!

One day while enjoying a swim at a hotel pool, I watched a man reading his book and thoroughly enjoying it. I thought, "How exciting it will be to look over and see a total stranger reading *my book!* The culmination of my life's purpose realized! Wow, after all these years of dreaming, planning, believing, and taking action—the manifestation of my dream! Creating something out of nothing and relishing the satisfaction of helping others grow from grunt to greatness."

It gave me chills just thinking about it!

As the months progressed, my thinking started to shift:
- What if nobody likes my book?
- Or it doesn't help them?
- *Who am I* to be writing a book?
- Am I being too personal?
- Do people really care?
- Will they laugh?

OR EVEN WORSE . . .

Chapter 7 — Overcome Fear

What if the book is a best seller and I get rich and famous and turn into a pompous jerk?

What if that guy at the swimming pool wants to talk to me and I just want to relax without interruption?

What if Oprah features my book on her show, then my printer can't handle all the orders that her endorsement generates? Or what if I say something stupid while on her interview couch?

Do I really want to be famous? What if my life changes too much?

Okay, before you think that I'm crazy, ask, "Have I ever had similar thoughts about my dreams?"

Thoughts like . . .

- "What if I become successful and my friends don't like me anymore?"
- "What if when I get in perfect shape I get cocky and look down on others?"
- "What if I get that promotion and my coworkers write me off?"
- "What if I am not as good a leader as I think I will be?"
- "What if I get a divorce?"

What are you afraid of?

Fear will wreck your pursuit of greatness in a hurry. It will keep you from believing in yourself, from thinking the right thoughts, from making powerful decisions, from dreaming, and most of all from taking action and manifesting your greatness.

A book that has changed my life is *Feel the Fear and Do It Anyway* by Susan Jeffers. I highly recommend you read it and implement its teachings.

For my part, I challenge you to realize that, as human beings, our greatest fear is not in making mistakes or failing, but that we actually might achieve our goals and dreams. *Then what?*

Chapter 7 — Overcome Fear

I have found no better passage about this fear than the following one written by Marianne Williamson. You may have read or heard it before, but today, let it sink in and plant meaningful roots in your mind.

> Our deepest fear is not that we are inadequate. Our deepest fear is that we are powerful beyond measure. It is our light, not our darkness that most frightens us. We ask ourselves, who am I to be brilliant, gorgeous, talented, and fabulous? Actually, who are you not to be? You are a child of God. Your playing small does not serve the world. There is nothing enlightened about shrinking so that other people won't feel insecure around you. We are all meant to shine, as children do. We were born to manifest the glory of God that is within us. It is not just in some of us; it is in everyone. And as we let our own light shine, we unconsciously give other people permission to do the same. As we are liberated from our own fear, our presence automatically liberates others.

Remember, *everyone* struggles with fear. You are not alone. Your job is to understand how fear holds you back. Love and laugh at yourself and keep pushing forward in pursuit of your greatness. **The pit in your stomach that comes from being too afraid to take action is far, far greater than the pain you might feel from failing or succeeding.**

Being a grunt by allowing fear to hold you back and being mediocre serves no one . . . not you, not your family, not your friends. Nor does it help you improve the quality of the world around you. Remember, you are the greatest miracle in the world. Start acting like it!

Oprah, I look forward to hearing from you. And I promise to be a great guest!

Dirty Little Secrets

A 59-year-old man dressed handsomely in a crisp blue suit and red tie strides to the microphone with confidence. Behind him is an American Flag and 20 of his closest friends, supporters, and advisors. His lovely wife and three children stand proudly beside him.

He speaks . . .

"My name is Gray Johnson from Massachusetts. I am running for President of the United States of America. I would like to share with you what qualifies me, and what I plan to do for you, the citizens of this great country of ours.

"But before I do, you should know a few things about me. And I'd rather you hear them from me, upfront and honest, than on the news or in the tabloids.

Chapter 7 — Overcome Fear

"I'm not perfect. I've made mistakes in my life. While I am not proud of them, and I believe they have no bearing on my ability to run this country with honor, I am not going to hide them from you.

"The first is that 17 years ago, during a difficult time in my marriage, I had an affair with another woman. It lasted three months.

"Secondly, I smoked marijuana in college and I did inhale. I probably smoked about 50 times from 1960 to 1964. I haven't smoked since then.

"And lastly, I rent adult videos from time to time."

Can you comprehend a presidential candidate being this honest? How *refreshing* it would be! I am willing to bet that if he were a candidate you liked—somebody you felt would lead this country well—you'd vote for Gray Johnson and not let his indiscretions hinder your decision. In fact, you'd probably respect him even more for honestly admitting them.

This is because you can relate to Gray Johnson.

In general, we don't identify and pursue our greatness because we are afraid—afraid because we feel inadequate. We feel inadequate because we feel ashamed—ashamed because we think we are the only ones who ever mess up.

Well, if you fall into this category, you're not the only one.

I have coached hundreds of people in one-on-one personal settings. Many have a "secret" that they don't want others to know about:

- Becky is having an affair.
- Tom spent time in jail for selling drugs.
- Peter hit his wife once.
- Sarah suffers from depression.
- John lost his license for drunk driving.
- Susan ran a red light in her car and killed a little boy.
- Donna was molested by her uncle.
- Peter is addicted to Vicoden.
- Don is in therapy for low self-esteem.

These are real clients of mine (names changed, of course). It's important to acknowledge that these are not bad people. *Each one of them and hundreds of others are intelligent, functioning, good, decent, honest, hard working, loving people.* And I would stake my life on the fact that 80 percent of the people reading this book suffer guilt because of one or more of these situations or similar ones.

Go ahead, name your secret.

I challenge you not to let your guilt, shame, or inadequacies get in the way of your greatness. Almost everyone feels guilty about something. Lead by example and show others through your actions that everyone is deserving and capable of enjoying the path to greatness!

When Great People Do Gruntish Things

The director of public relations for the San Francisco 49ers football team resigned after producing a "sensitivity" training video for the team that included racial slurs and topless dancers. Can you comprehend why an otherwise professional man would do such a gruntish thing?

This is not uncommon. People around us do things like this all the time. They sabotage themselves.

Have you ever sabotaged your own success?

Take a moment and call to mind two to three instances when you have sabotaged your success. Perhaps you backed out of a new relationship just as it was really starting to go well because you feared making a commitment. Or, maybe you stopped working out as you began to lose weight. Or stopped marketing, just as your business began to grow.

Self-sabotage happens for two main reasons, one positive and the other destructive.

We use "destructive self-sabotage" to regulate our comfort zones. Whether you realize it or not, you have a picture of what you think you *deserve* in each area of your life. And if you start to surpass that level of comfort, your subconscious will self-correct and bring you back down.

It's important not to get down on yourself if this happens. Rather, learn from it. To prevent this, constantly strive to expand your self-love, and belief in yourself. You are a miracle, therefore you deserve and can handle more than you currently believe you can. If you maintain a level of appreciation, gratitude, deservedness, and respect for where you are while constantly expanding your standards and building your belief muscle, you will reduce your chances of self-destruction.

"Positive self-sabotage" is when God intervenes and helps you in creative ways. This happens because you fear taking action on your own and need a push. God knows you will grow through challenges, and while His influence may seemingly have a negative impact at first, it proves to produce a positive result in the long run. It is important for your future belief and confidence to view your self-sabotage in a positive way.

Here's an example of "positive" self-sabotage.

Chapter 7 — Overcome Fear

The Other Half Of The Story . . .

Remember Chapter 2 opened with the story of a guy lying in bed having heart palpitations because he was discontent and unsatisfied at work? He longed for the courage to pursue his dreams. You caught that this person was me, right? Now let me tell you the other half of the story.

That night, lying in bed soaked with sweat and breathing heavily, I made a decision to pursue my innermost dream . . .

Well, you didn't get the whole truth in Chapter 2. I did make a decision in that moment, but needed help to make my dream happen.

A year after making the decision to start my own coaching business, I was still managing the country club. I gained 15 more pounds and started dating one of my managers on the sly because we didn't want the members and the company to know about it. Once a terrific manager of people and a caring, patient boss, I began treating employees and members curtly and losing my patience.

In the background, I had begun to research coaching and speaking, but wasn't ready to make the leap, resign, and start my own business. I was scared.

About this time, I suddenly felt it important to begin a hobby I had been thinking about for years—painting. I painted an abstract, yet sensual picture and hung it in

From *Grunt* to GREATNESS!

my home along with the other paintings I had created. At some point later, I had a house party and invited some members of my management team. About six months after that, I terminated a female manager (and one of the party attendees) for poor performance. She sued me for sexual harassment, citing that my painting and subsequent verbal description of it made her feel very uncomfortable at the party. Of course, I knew nothing about this at the time. She never expressed her discomfort or asked for an apology. She didn't even leave the party early, but continued to enjoy herself.

Every person I've told this story to has defended me, saying her suit was ridiculous and she had no case. Maybe so, but please understand that it came as a tumultuous, devastating blow to me. I felt dirty, guilty, and ashamed.

Happily, everything worked out OK. My company settled, I got a reprimand, and the dust cleared. But you know how baby birds often need to be pushed from the nest so they can spread their wings and fly? *Well, this became my big push from the nest!*

After some thought and analysis, I saw my spiraling self-sabotage as a sign from God. I had lost interest in my work and had to leave the company to pursue my dreams, so I resigned. And while I've had my share of challenges since then, starting my own business was the best decision I ever made in my life.

Chapter 7 — Overcome Fear

Have you ever done seemingly stupid things, acting in a manner inconsistent with your true, typical self? Are you doing that in some way right now? Perhaps you are:

- Putting on weight
- Showing up late for work
- Treating employees or coworkers poorly
- Spending money you don't have
- Skipping your worship routine
- Getting into fights with your spouse or friends for no real reason

Do you need a push out of your nest?

I challenge you to examine what you are doing that might be out of character and ask yourself why. Are you sabotaging yourself because you're afraid of your greatness? And/or might God be helping you make a decision that you can't seem to make on your own?

Is it time to leave that dead-end job or your unfulfilling marriage? Are you ready to start that business you've been dreaming of? Is it time to finally have the peace, joy, and self-satisfaction you deserve?

Don't shrink from your greatness; discover it! You deserve more. Lead by example and show others what greatness looks and feels like so they, too, will have the courage to pursue their goals and dreams!

8

Take Plaction!

*Have a bias toward action—
let's see something happen now.
You can break that big plan into small steps
and take the first step right away.*

— Indira Gandhi

In Michael Gerber's wildly successful books *The E-Myth: Why Most Small Businesses Don't Work and What to Do About It* and *E-Myth Revisited,* he challenged entrepreneurs to work *on* their business, not *in* their business.

He wrote that most entrepreneurs are "technicians suffering from an entrepreneurial seizure!" In his humorous yet powerful talks, he declares that they are too busy "doin' it, doin' it, doin' it" to step back and act like owners of their business.

This applies to our lives too. Especially in today's technologically advanced, hyper-speed environment, we can get so busy doing, doing, doing; going, going, going; moving, moving, moving, that we rarely take a step back and ask two important questions: "What am I doing here?" and "Why?"

~

Are you too busy working *in* your life, rather than *on* your life?

Are you creating a proactive life—a life of intention, purpose, and self-discovery? Or are you too busy reacting, responding, and being tossed around on the boat of life?

Now that you have identified what greatness means to you in each area of the Umbrella of Life, it is now time to *plan* how you're going to pursue your greatness, and take *action*. I call this PLACTION!

A Simple Plan

Determining what greatness means to you and creating your vision was the act of defining what you *want*. Forming a plan requires deciding what you *do* to pursue your greatness.

Naturally, the complexity of your plans will depend on your goals and dreams. Starting a business, for example, requires more planning that losing 15 pounds. For now, I suggest you focus on the area of your life that you most want to improve right now. What is your plan, or what is it you need to do to achieve greatness ?

Chapter 8 — Take Plaction!

In the arena of health, part of your plan might be to hire a personal trainer, or to train for a marathon, or create and execute a weight training and aerobic exercise schedule.

In the panel of finance, your plan might consist of consolidating your credit card debt, meeting with a financial advisor, or setting up automatic payroll deduction.

In family, your plan might consist of incorporating a "date night" once a week with your wife, and/or committing to do homework with your daughter for one hour each night, or volunteering at your child's school.

You know what you want in each area of your life, and if you give it thought, I bet you know what you need to do, too. The biggest challenge is to actually do it!

Think it. Plan it. Do it.

This expression says it all: "Those who fail to plan, plan to fail." I totally agree and will add this caveat: "Those who plan too much are grunts."

Okay, I'm no Emerson. But my point is this: The main purpose of planning is to get you to take action. When people don't plan, they lose out on the specific, targeted, focused action that they've deemed important to reach greatness. When people plan too much, they get so caught up in planning that they become paralyzed and don't take action. If I had to pick one, I'd take a person who *does* over a person who simply *plans* any day of the week.

From *Grunt* to GREATNESS!

A mantra in sales says, "Nothing happens until somebody sells something." That implies that the success of every business is contingent on sales. Someone can create the greatest product or service in the world and it doesn't mean a hill of beans until people buy it!

Well, I'd like to modify this axiom to say: **Nothing happens until you do something.**

The world has no shortage of people with great ideas . . . big dreams, meaningful intentions, and strong desires.

But, a riddle asks: "Where are hundreds of thousands of the world's most amazing dreams and ideas stored?

The answer? In cemeteries. Here lie the most wonderful array of unfulfilled dreams, untried ideas, and unrealized passions. They are buried forever with the people who were too afraid to take action!

What dreams or desires do you have?

When are you going to DO something about your dreams and desires? What the hell are you waiting for? Quit patting yourself on the back for simply having a dream or a great idea. DO something with it! Take action!

Action is what separates:
- the men from the boys,
- the haves from the have-nots,

Chapter 8 — Take Plaction!

- the doers from the talkers,
- the greats from the grunts!

Are you ready?

When you're ready, please visit www.fromgrunttogreatness.com to sign up for a complimentary "action planning" group. We offer these groups free as a thank you for reading this book and to support you in your quest for greatness. These "telegroups" are conducted over the phone, so you can enjoy them from the comfort of your office or living room. We look forward to serving you.

Cranking and Grinding

Often when my buddy Dave calls, he starts the conversation by asking, "Are you cranking or grinding today?" He's mocking me because I use these terms frequently and he can never remember which is which.

"Cranking" happens when you're getting a lot done. You're committed, focused, and TAKING ACTION with little distraction—no procrastination or second-guessing.

"Grinding" occurs when you're actively getting through the day in spite of the challenges you face at every turn. Maybe things aren't going your way or you're distracted, but you *keep hanging in there and work diligently to maintain your concentration to get things accomplished.*

This term was born after I heard Tiger Woods and other professional golfers talk about "grinding it out." That's when they're not "in the zone"—not making the exceptional shots—but they're getting through the round with few mistakes and *setting the stage for a better day tomorrow.*

Are you a cranker and a grinder?

Do you grind it out when you are struggling, or do you pack it in and give up? How many crank days do you have in a week? Would you agree that somebody who cranks and grinds will achieve greatness over somebody who doesn't? **The more you crank and grind, the sooner you will achieve your goals!** *And, you will relish a sense of satisfaction and pride that comes from the discipline required to crank and grind . . . even when you don't feel like it.*

Break Free From Your Bondage

In one of my favorite movies "The Shawshank Redemption," Andy Dufresne (played by Tim Robbins) is sentenced to prison for two life sentences. He spent 19 years in the astounding feat of escaping from prison. Do you remember how he did it? He used a tiny rock hammer, small enough to fit in the palm of his hand. Painfully and excruciatingly slowly, he picked through 50 feet of crumbling wall over a 19-year period. He gathered the bits of wall and rock, put them in his pocket, and spread the debris throughout the jail yard during social time. He then crawled through 500 yards of sewage pipe to his freedom.

Chapter 8 — Take Plaction!

Morgan Freeman, the film's narrator, remarked that "Andy loved geology. *Geology after all is the study of pressure and time.*"

It took Andy 19 years to achieve freedom. He applied pressure for a long, long time.

Greatness also takes pressure and time. To achieve your most treasured goals and dreams, you must be constantly applying pressure (taking action) over the course of time . . . sometimes months and years.

What are you willing to do for your greatness?
What are you willing to do to achieve your liberation, your freedom, your fulfillment, your happiness, your goals and dreams?

From *Grunt* to GREATNESS!

Growing from grunt to greatness takes constant and never-ending pressure and time; it takes consistent, persistent, daily, weekly, monthly, and yearly action. Challenge yourself to enjoy the process of achieving greatness!

White Teeth Take Time

What is the deal with kids today? Have you noticed how incredibly straight and white their teeth are? Just take a good look at four or five teenagers the next time you're in the mall on a Saturday afternoon. Their teeth look so perfectly white, straight, and large, they seem like one big tooth—like the mouthpiece a boxer wears!

In the late '70s, when I was 13 years old, my mom took me to the dentist to explore whether or not I needed braces. After a full examination, he told her that my bite was perfect and that I had no need for braces other than for cosmetic reasons. Since I grew up in a middle-income family and my parents were the furthest thing from vain, they didn't purchase braces for me.

Now, 25 years later, I still have a perfect bite and no cavities, but as a coach and public speaker, I want my teeth to look whiter and straighter. Curious and determined, I met with my dentist to learn about teeth whitening. He told me that the procedure entails four one-hour bleaching sessions in his office, followed by 21 days of wearing in-home whitening trays for eight hours while sleeping.

Chapter 8 — Take Plaction!

Well, typical me, after wearing the trays for three nights in a row, I started looking for signs of whiter teeth all day long. Every time I got within five feet of a mirror or any other reflective surface (microwave door, car window, shiny office building), I'd check out my teeth! I not only looked at them straight on, but I looked from every angle at different times of the day and in various conditions . . . direct sunlight, in fluorescent lighting, in semi-darkness. Hell, I even tried to sneak a glimpse of my mouth while walking by a mirror to see if I could notice whiter teeth when not really "looking!"

After three days of this, my teeth didn't look like Tom Cruise's. So what did I do?

I stopped.

Now, eight months later, I'm still reminded of my gruntness when I see the unused whitening gel syringes and teeth molds on my vanity counter. I stubbornly refuse to put them away because *tonight* I am going to start using them again!

Where do you see signs of giving up too soon?
Do you look for the short cut, the quick fix, the easy solution, and stop before your work has a chance to take hold?

How long have you been working out and eating right in order to lose weight? Have you gone to the gym three to

From *Grunt* to GREATNESS!

four times a week for the past year? Or have you been on a diet for a week and are now frustrated that you haven't lost 10 pounds?

Have you really given your business enough time to evolve and blossom into a thriving, well-oiled machine? Have you done all that's required or are you being a grunt and griping about how long it takes?

Have you dedicated yourself to finding your soul mate: asking friends to set you up, joining online dating services, going on blind dates, introducing yourself to new people? Or are you watching TV at night, eating popcorn, and wondering why nobody's calling you?

The dentist told me to use the whitening trays eight hours every night for 21 days for a reason. I only used them for 14 percent of that time and I wonder why my teeth aren't looking like pearls yet? What a grunt I can be.

Do You Have the Discipline It Takes?

Recall a time when you completely dedicated yourself to a worthwhile goal. Perhaps you trained for a marathon or followed an intense 12-week workout program or completed a six-month project at work or adhered to a year-long plan to get out of debt, quit smoking, or even write a book.

How did you feel during this heightened period of discipline, dedication, and self-control? I guarantee that if

Chapter 8 — Take Plaction!

you're being honest with yourself, you'll admit the process was one of the most liberating, satisfying, proud periods of your life. And remember, I am not talking about the *attainment* of the goal. I am talking about the *process* to get there. C'mon, admit it. You loved it!

∼

I challenge you to incorporate these principles of discipline, self-control, self-respect, and self-LOVE into your life. Enjoy the rush of doing so and relish its rewards!

Patience Soup

One day in 1998 while working at the country club, I was having lunch with my membership director Sylvia Jackson. Sylvia, who has since died, was wise beyond her years, and a loving and compassionate teacher. I was complaining about my struggles and how long it was apparently taking me to evolve as a leader.

She leaned in and said, "Let's say you had all the ingredients for a lovely soup in a big bowl—tomatoes, beans, chicken, celery, noodles, chicken broth, salt, pepper, water. Imagine you just prepared them and they're all just sitting there in a bowl, not yet on the stove. Is this soup?"

"No, not yet. It's just a pot of ingredients," I replied. "Exactly," she said. *"You have all the makings of a delicious soup. You just have to let it simmer for a while."*

I will never forget this lesson. In a one-minute story, Sylvia told me more about patience than I had learned in my lifetime. And she instilled a needed sense of peace in me. As a result, I no longer doubted my ability, my skills, or my belief in myself. I saw that I had all the ingredients of a great soup. I just had to let the ingredients simmer, evolving and combining over time.

You, too, have all the ingredients of greatness. I challenge you to take action and make your soup! And balance this action with a confident sense of patience as you enjoy the journey to greatness.

9

Get Coached

Three billion people on the face of the earth go to bed hungry every night, but four billion people go to bed every night hungry for a simple word of encouragement and recognition.

— Cavett Robert,
Founder National Speakers Association

A Tony Robbins seminar at the L.A. Convention Center a few years ago was an awesome experience. Tony had 3,000 people so fired up, inspired, and confident that it felt like the arena would explode. I called my girlfriend on the way home to tell her how much my life was going to change.

Can you relate to this?

Reflect upon a time when you listened to a powerful audio program, read a great book, or saw an inspirational speaker. Get connected to when you made a decision to make a big change in your life and committed to pursue a significant goal and dream once and for all.

- Have you implemented all that you learned in that seminar, tape, or book?
- How much has your life *really* changed for the better as a result?
- Have you lost the weight you intended to lose?
- Have you made the millions you said you would?
- Are you the husband or the wife you really want to be?
- Did you quit that job and start your own business?
- Is your business as successful as you wanted it to be?

If so, good for you. I am genuinely happy for you and congratulate you. Most of us, however, need something more.

And that something is personal coaching.

To be honest, I was hesitant to include this section for fear of sounding self-serving. After all, coaching is a large part of what my company provides. But in order to best serve you on your journey to greatness, it would be *negligent to not firmly recommend partnering with a coach to help you reach your most cherished goals and dreams.*

Working with my own personal coaches for more than seven years has changed my life. You certainly have heard about my gruntness in this book. But much of it I have overcome, in large part due to the support of my coaches.

Chapter 9 — Get Coached

From dropping 30 pounds and getting healthy, to creating a very successful business that allows me to travel around the world and work from wherever I please, coaching has changed my life.

And I am even more happy that my coaching of others has had a profound impact on many lives.

Quite simply, if you are really dedicated to achieving greatness in any area of your life, you need to work with a coach.

But why? Well, coaching works for four main reasons. A coach . . .

Provides Expertise — The best coaches specialize in a particular area. They combine their knowledge of self-help with a particular expertise, such as health and wellness, small business growth, or marriage dynamics. This 1-2 punch combines the best of consulting and psychology to help you achieve your goals.

Holds You To Higher Standards — A coach will hold you to higher standards. This book is about greatness. A coach will help you define, pursue and achieve a higher level of success and greatness than you ever dreamed you could. Coaches demand, request, and cajole excellence out of you, even when you are not feeling like being your best!

Keeps You Accountable and In Action — A great coach helps hold you accountable. You may know exactly what you need to do to achieve your desired level of greatness in each area. The challenge, however, isn't always in the knowing "what to do" or "how to do it," but in actually *DOING what we know we need to be doing* in order to achieve greatness. This is what coaches do best. Simply, the best coaches can get you to take more action than you would on your own.

Helps Strengthen Your Belief — And lastly, as the quotation above suggests, a coach listens to you, strategizes with you, and provides you with the support, love, and encouragement you need to pursue greatness. This strengthens your belief and confidence. As we've said throughout this book, success is not easy and you will face many obstacles. A coach will help build your resolve through these challenging times and remind you of what greatness tastes, looks, and feels like and why you embarked on this terrific journey!

You obviously are dedicated to your success or you would not have purchased this book or read this far. I urge you to go the extra mile and commit to hiring a coach.

Of course, I'd like you to consider our *FGTG* coaches because they are trained on the principles of this book. They were selected because they are the best and they each specialize in a specific panel of the *Umbrella Of Life*.

Please visit www.coachfederation.org to learn more about hiring a coach. Please visit www.fromgrunttogreatness.com to schedule a complimentary consultation with a coach, and buckle up for the ride to greatness!

10

Expect To Be Challenged

I think a hero is an ordinary individual who finds strength to persevere and endure in spite of overwhelming obstacles.

— Christopher Reeve

As part of my own journey from grunt to greatness, I seek to enhance my relationship with God, and decided to kill two birds with one stone by attending a relationship series put on by the singles ministry at my local church. Why not learn about how to have a strong marriage and meet wonderful single women at the same time?

One class about "relationship busters" featured self-centeredness as its first "buster." I agreed and certainly know that too much focus on oneself hinders a relationship from blossoming. The second relationship buster was cohabitation prior to marriage. Hmmmm, that one was tough. I had always thought that living with someone before marriage might be a good way to determine if a marriage could work.

The third relationship buster was pre-marital sex. After a balanced and articulate presentation on the negatives of pre-marital sex, the pastor issued this challenge: "By a show of hands, how many of you will commit right now to not engage in sex until you are married?" Every single person in the room of 28 raised his or her hand. That is, except for me.

Now, it would have been easy to raise my hand without much thought, but I didn't want to lie. The right side of my neck knotted up. I began to sweat. While I respected his belief, I felt stressed and couldn't accept his challenge. When the class ended, I left and never went back. Now, I am not saying that I should have necessarily accepted his challenge; however, I am not pleased with the way in which I handled the situation . . . by simply "checking out" and not returning.

What do you do when you are challenged?

Do you lean in, dig deep, and reach for your ability to rise to the occasion? Or do you step back, retreat, and check out?

Expect to be stretched. You will have setbacks. The pursuit of greatness is not necessarily easy. As I said earlier, this is about the journey and no instant solution exists. As you grow and take action, you will run into barriers.

Many people feel ashamed of their challenges or setbacks. They think they are the only ones who struggle. They observe "the greats" and incorrectly determine that they don't

Chapter 10 — Expect To Be Challenged

struggle, and therefore feel they themselves aren't destined for greatness.

Yet everybody struggles. Everybody "checks out" from time to time. My challenge to you is to love yourself as you are, embrace your gruntness, AND strive to improve your discipline and self-control. When you do, you'll reduce the volume and intensity of your "check out" times.

To the extent that we can genuinely laugh off our struggles, challenges, and failures, we have achieved a level of greatness. Think about it. When you strongly desire something and truly believe that you will have it and keep taking action even in the face of adversity, do you think you will eventually achieve what you want?

When you get down to it, your ability to overcome failures and not give up is the key to your success. And if you can be unattached to or unaffected by your challenges— even laugh at them—then you will keep taking action. That's the key!

Dried Apples and McDonald's

My friend Nikki and I had just run eight miles. It was week six of our marathon training with Coach Matt. (By the way, if you are thinking about running a marathon, I highly recommend *Team in Training*. Check them out at www.teamintraining.org.)

From *Grunt* to GREATNESS!

Back to the story . . . We were soaked to the bone, sore, and drained, but euphoric after an intense run in the Palos Verdes hills on an early Saturday morning in June.

It was a particularly rough run for me. I never quite rebounded from the intense two-mile uphill climb that began the run. I felt winded throughout and my hamstrings were tight as a drum. I was convinced that my labor was due to my continued struggle with diet.

Mind you, I had just run eight miles! How many people can pop off eight miles by 8:30 a.m. on a Saturday morning? Yet, due to the difficulty of the run, and the snugness of my water pack around my waist, I was feeling like a grunt.

I asked Nikki about her nutrition routine. After all, she completed the eight miles with ease 15 minutes ahead of me.

"Oh, wow," she exclaimed. "I really struggle with my nutrition. It's a constant battle. I absolutely die for those dried apples from Whole Foods. Sometimes I eat a whole bag at one time. I just can't stop!"

Nikki is one of the coolest people I know. She was not exaggerating in any way, nor was she being condescending. She was genuinely sharing her struggles and concerns about what she considered to be poor eating habits.

Somehow, though, I just couldn't muster the sympathy she was looking for. You see, my struggle with food at the

Chapter 10 — Expect To Be Challenged

time translated to that good old standby, the Super Size #4 at McDonald's or a medium Domino's pizza with lots of red meat and extra cheese. Compare that to a handful of dried apples and it's not hard to see why eight miles was easier for Nikki than it was for me!

Even though I had difficulty relating to her frustration with the dried apples, I realized that our struggles with gruntness and achievements of greatness are relative and personal to us. Nikki's challenge with dried apples, although seemingly ridiculous to me, is as much of a struggle for her as my McDonalds runs are to me. In further discussion, she explained other temptations, such as indulging in four slices of thin crust vegetarian pizza, or too much diet coke, or a pint of ice cream every six months. Oh, how I shudder at the thought!

But her challenges to excel in health and fitness are mentally the same as mine, just on a different level. She said she suffers from guilt and shame and vows to do better next time, just like I do.

What is your hidden weakness?
Remember, striving for greatness and overcoming gruntness are personal and relative. It's your responsibility to challenge yourself to evolve and get better in all areas of your life—to strive for your personal best. It doesn't matter what other people struggle with. Have compassion for them and understand that we are all the same, struggling and striving to be the best we can be. Isn't life grand?

From *Grunt* to GREATNESS!

I'm Not Lance Armstrong

Even prior to his overcoming cancer, I have always admired Lance Armstrong. He must be the fittest, most dedicated, focused, disciplined, and well-trained athlete in the world.

Yet for the longest time, I avoided reading his book, *It's Not About the Bike*.

I couldn't read his book because I couldn't relate to him. His dedication to nutrition and training, his single-minded focus, plus his incredible discipline went beyond my comprehension. I decided he couldn't possibly be a great husband or father because he has to spend so much time training. I determined that I really wouldn't want to be like him.

I was ashamed about by my feelings toward Lance and people like him. Two of my best friends are incredibly fit, dedicated, disciplined, and passionate runners. I, on the other hand (prior to my marathon), couldn't run straight from my apartment to the corner fast food joint without feeling like I was going to have a heart attack! It was difficult to be around Dan and Dave, and to read about people like Lance, because being around them "held up a mirror" to me and made me feel inadequate. I didn't like what I saw in comparison to them. Rather than being inspired to take action and pursue my fitness dreams, I felt paralyzed. It was easier to make excuses for my bad habits and not push myself more to improve my physical condition.

Chapter 10 — Expect To Be Challenged

Have you ever felt inferior?

Have you ever felt this way in any area of your life? Is it ever difficult for you to be around people who have what you want and whom you believe are superior to you in a particular area?

I finally decided to look within as well as survey others to learn what this was all about. What I discovered was this: *If the gap or disparity between a role model and you is too wide, it might lead to paralysis on your part.*

In my case, rather than learning from Lance, Dave, or Dan, I became frustrated and angry with myself for being so far removed from them. So, rather than "leaning in," I would retreat and become paralyzed. I'd say, "Why bother?"

Can you relate to this?

One morning, while preparing to speak at a conference in Tucson, I was talking with one of the attendees. She mentioned that she loves a particular world-renowned motivational speaker, but prefers his "older stuff" to what he teaches now. When asked why, she said, "I could relate more when he was discussing his fears and challenges that were the same as mine. Now he's a multimillionaire and I can't relate anymore."

I hope that *From Grunt To Greatness* appeals to the grunt in all of us. When you read about my struggles, I hope you will say, "That sounds like me, and if he can do it, so can I!"

From *Grunt* to GREATNESS!

And you can!

Who do you admire?

I believe in and recommend role models. Study the people who you believe are successful at doing the things you want to do and being the type of person you want to be. You don't have to become them, but consider modeling some of their effective actions while incorporating your uniqueness.

Be careful, however, not to become paralyzed. It is important to remember that your role models are no better than you overall. They just might be better than you in a particular area.

So you must know yourself. The only way is through observation and reflection, looking deep within and making adjustments through trial and error. Does the gap between you and your role models inspire you or paralyze you?

Chapter 10 — Expect To Be Challenged

By the way, I finally read Lance's book and learned a great deal from him, and I am happy being me, just as Lance, Dave, and Dan would want it.

Manage Expectations

My assistant and sister-in-law, Julie, and I had been meeting every Friday morning at 7:00 a.m. to review our accounting, client billing, bank reconciliation, and so on. One morning a few years ago, I was feeling agitated and frustrated as we reviewed our revenues. Finally Julie asked, "What the heck is the matter with you today, Mr. Crabby?"

"I'm so sick and tired of struggling with this business," I shot back. "When the hell is it going to get easier?"

"What are you talking about, you goober? I thought you were going to be psyched. It's only September and you have exceeded last year's revenues. And the winter is your strongest quarter."

Later, I reflected upon my agitation. While she was absolutely correct in her positive thoughts, it gave me little solace. The reason? My revenues were 30 percent short of where I *wanted them to be* at the time. My goal was to double revenues from the previous year. It was becoming clear that wasn't going to happen, so I was feeling frustrated and disappointed.

I bet you can see where I'm going with this. Double my revenues? What was I thinking? I was feeling like a grunt for falling short of my expectation, rather than feeling great for exceeding last year's revenues by 70 percent!

I love that Julie can find the good in anything. While I wanted to dwell on my shortcomings, she coaxed me into celebrating my improvement over the previous year. Who's the personal coach here anyway?

∼

When you set goals and expectations, it is important to do so carefully and realistically.

Have you ever been frustrated for losing "only" two pounds in a week because you wanted to lose five? Perhaps you reduced your debt this year by 20 percent, but you believe you failed because you wanted to cut it in half. Are you beating yourself up because you missed your daughter's recital, yet still improved your attendance at her school events over last year? Have you started attending church on a more regular basis, but feel like a sinner when you don't go every week?

Are you recognizing your successes along the way?
Manage your goals and expectations carefully. **Be good to yourself and strive for "constant improvement," not perfection.** *Set expectations, sure, but use them as a mechanism to get you to act and improve, because you may not always hit the target.*

Chapter 10 — Expect To Be Challenged

In your evolution from grunt to greatness, you will face thousands of challenges, big and small, physical and emotional. Some you will overcome like a champion and others you will wrestle with and feel like a grunt. This applies to everyone—*and it will always be this way.* So, enjoy the journey. It's a lot more fun that way.

From *Grunt* to GREATNESS!

11

Don't Give Up (Maybe)

"There are better writers and directors than me who are working at Burger King. They gave up too early. It took me 12 years before I could make a living directing."

— Frank Darabont,
Director of The Shawshank Redemption,
The Green Mile, and others

Do these sayings sound familiar?

- "When the going gets tough, the tough get going."
- "I can see the light at the end of the tunnel."
- "You're almost to the finish line . . . just keep going."
- "Go for it . . . grab the brass ring."

Have you ever been to a seminar, read a self-help book, listened to an audio program, or heard a great speech that conveyed the message to give up the pursuit of your dreams?

- "Throw in the towel, buddy."
- "Give it up."
- "Nice try, but move on."
- "It ain't going to happen."
- "Don't quit your day job."

The people writing the books, recording the CDs, and giving the speeches are doing them now because they hung in; they've accomplished their goals and dreams. They can look back and draw from their experience to advise you to do what worked for them.

But what about the people who have given it their all and failed?

Did John Kerry and Bob Dole try hard to become president? What about the Olympic athletes who train for months and years for that "one shot," but fall short of the gold, or even the bronze and silver?

How about you?

Is there anything you worked your tail off for, but it just didn't happen?

Take a moment and call to mind something you really wanted, committed to go after it, really believed you could do it, and did everything in your power to achieve it, but it just didn't work out.

Chapter 11 — Don't Give Up (Maybe)

Is there anything you are working on now that doesn't seem to be coming together the way you believe it should? Should you keep going?

Maybe . . . maybe not.

When Quitting is the Answer

When do you give up and when do you stay the course and continue pursuing your dreams?

What if the Olympic athlete never wins the gold, or the Cubbies the World Series? What if I never appear on Oprah? What if you don't ever get that dream house, have the ideal marriage, or build the thriving business?

Do you quit?

As a self-help coach for seven years, I continue to struggle with this question. The best answer I can come up with is that you hang in there until one or all three of the following things happen:

1. You genuinely no longer want the goal or dream.

2. You completely lose all belief and confidence in ever achieving it.

3. What you are sacrificing in pursuit exceeds what you are willing to give and thus diminishes your happiness.

And to be clear, we're not talking about having a couple of bad days or even weeks. I mean when months pass and you find yourself hating what you're doing, or you realize it's just not worth the struggle anymore.

I most admire successful people who achieve a sense of balance and fullness in their lives, even if it means giving up a little bit of their potential in one area. Remember our definition of greatness: To enjoy peace of mind and happiness by loving yourself now, and pursuing balanced personal potential in each area—the umbrella of your life.

Balance is a key component. Be careful not to pursue greatness in one area while neglecting all others.

It's who you become in the process

Yet, before you give up the pursuit of a dream, remember it is not always about the destination, but who you become in the process.

A client named Debbie had been creating terrific art her whole life, and in the last year in particular. She was thinking the right thoughts, committed to her vision of selling art, and creating beautiful pieces.

But they weren't selling.

Understandably, she was getting increasingly frustrated, so she sent me a letter asking for the "the secret" and suggesting that she should quit or at least change her medium

Chapter 11 — Don't Give Up (Maybe)

to produce paintings more like Dennis Hopper's, who was successfully selling his artwork.

Even though Debbie was not selling paintings, her life was evolving dramatically. Due to her focus, dedication, and belief in her work, she'd become more patient with her children and more loving toward her husband. Gone were her severe migraines and other ailments. She was more passionate, healthy, and "alive" than ever before.

The Secret

This letter I wrote to her conveys my philosophy:

Dear Debbie,

You are exactly where you are supposed to be with your art and everything else in your life. You are on the path. You need not second-guess your actions. You see, it is the journey that is the reward. Look at who you are becoming in pursuit of your goals and dreams. This is it! The selling of art is not only what you are after. It is a goal to allow you to evolve from the inside as you move toward it.

Would you trade your growth during the last few years for the sale of 20 paintings? I bet and hope not. The great thing is this: your paintings will get sold as a result of your evolution. But, you must allow yourself to grow and evolve *for you*, not just to sell your paintings.

Look at you! What part of you is remotely similar to the person you were two years ago? I say virtually nothing: your art, your face, your body, your mind, your house, your relationship with your family, your thinking, your health, and on and on.

In the beginning, you said goals have a funny way of coming true. Keep setting them, keep creating action steps, keep evaluating, adopting, and adjusting—all good and very important actions, crucial in fact. But never lose sight of what is happening right before our eyes, in part, as a result of this work. This is the beauty. This is the secret!

Mike

I am happy to report that Debbie did adopt this philosophy of focusing on her evolution *as a person* vs. simply selling her paintings. Now, three years later she has sold several paintings; and, in addition, she is the artist who created Griffin. So the secret really works! Isn't she great?

Chapter 11 — Don't Give Up (Maybe)

Frogs Really DO Pay Off!

Not boiling frogs this time . . . prosperity frogs! In Eastern cultures, frogs are believed to bring prosperity. Feng Shui experts recommend placing decorative frogs throughout your home to bring financial abundance.

When Julie learned this, she bought me some frogs.

About three months later, my company had the biggest month ever financially. In one of our meetings, Julie said, "See, those frogs I got you are really paying off!" God bless her—once again, the eternal optimist. But she got me thinking. Did the frogs bring this prosperity? Or was it the huge marketing campaign we just did? Or the new division we created? Or working our butts off? Or thinking the right thoughts? Or believing in ourselves? Or serving others? Or five years of hard work finally paying off?

Or maybe it was the frogs . . . Hey, whatever it takes!

From *Grunt* to GREATNESS!

Principle of convergence

I'd venture that it was all the above, or a concept I call *convergence*. This is when you do all the things outlined in this book and get the results you're looking for. *Does having a dream come true depend on any one step or all of the steps?*

Although saying this seems paradoxical to the ideas at the beginning of this chapter, if you apply the steps and principles outlined in this book, you *will* achieve your goals and dreams. You will evolve from grunt to greatness. You will become a better person. You will enjoy and relish the fruits of your labor.

Remember, if you have the ability to visualize what you want, and you believe you can manifest this dream, then you can. Otherwise you would have not been given the ability to visualize it in the first place.

The fact that God gave you the desire to start a business, be a phenomenal parent and spouse, or achieve financial abundance means that you *can* do it. You "just" have to follow all the steps in this book!

And filling your home with prosperity frogs can't hurt either!

12

Enjoy The Journey

Every day you may make progress. Every step may be fruitful. Yet there will stretch out before you an ever-lengthening, ever-ascending, ever-improving path. You know you will never get to the end of the journey. But this, so far from discouraging, only adds to the joy and glory of the climb.

— Sir Winston Churchill

Old Milwaukee Said It Best!

Just envision three paunchy middle-aged men, unshaven and unkempt, huddled together in a small rowboat in the middle of a lake on a hot afternoon. It's humid, sticky and the air smells of dead fish bait. The three guys are smoking cheap cigars and drinking Old Milwaukee Beer at $1.99 a six-pack. One of them, with a big grin on his face, stands up with arms outstretched and says, "Does it get any better than this?"

From *Grunt* to GREATNESS!

I remember seeing that beer commercial as a kid and thinking, "I sure as hell hope so. If that's as good as it gets, just shoot me right now!" Well, of course I was half joking, but I sure as heck get the message now.

My friends sometimes poke fun at me because it seems that whatever we are doing at that moment is "the best in my life." Lots of times, they have heard me exclaim things like:

- "That was the best five iron I ever hit in my life!"
- "This is *literally* the BEST piece of salmon I've ever eaten!"
- "I have never enjoyed a cigar as much as this one, right here, right now."

And the thing is . . . *I really mean it!* While I may have hit the best five-iron shot, enjoyed the perfect piece of salmon, and smoked the best cigar before, *right here, right now,* these are the best. And it doesn't get any better than this. (Until next time, of course!)

How happy are you with the way things are? **Can you pursue what you want in the future while being grateful for the way things are right now?**

Chapter 12 — Enjoy the Journey

Presidents' Day

One Sunday in Torrance, California, I was in the back corner of Starbucks working on (what else) this book. With my earplugs in and my head down, I was tuning out everything and everyone around me.

Five hours later, while writing this section on mindfulness, I challenged myself to be even more "in the moment." Looking around the café, I noticed for the first time all day, that the entire wall next to me was filled with dozens of pictures of Abraham Lincoln and George Washington. As a sign told me, these pictures were colored by the K-2 students of Mrs. Gloyne's class at Walteria Elementary in Torrance, in celebration of Presidents' Day. A caption below each answered the question about what the respective presidents meant to them. Many of the students wrote the same thing. Here is a compilation of every one of their answers, word-for-word:

- "Abraham Lincoln was tall," "very tall," "a good man," "a very nice man," "a nice tall man," "wore all black."
- "George Washington is on the dollar bill," "lived a long time ago," "was a kind man," "traveled," "took care of himself in the woods," "was a nice man," "was a leader in the army."

Sitting there in Starbucks, I teared up as I pictured Mrs. Gloyne and these terrific kids working on their precious project. Awash in memories of my youth, I was thankful for yet another reminder to enjoy what's perfect and beautiful in front of me "in the moment."

Thank you, Mrs. Gloyne and Kate, Trevor, Madeline, Lauren, Olivia, Maisie, Skyler, A.M., Darell, Justin, Jordan, Kahta, Georgia, Sarah, Tommy, Eddie, and Allan.

Thank you for helping me—and my readers— remember to *balance the pursuit of a better future with what's perfect and beautiful now.*

A mini-meditation

Where are you as you read this book? Close your eyes for a moment and be mindful of your surroundings. If you're in a café, relish the energy from those around you. Breathe in the smell of freshly brewed coffee.

Perhaps you are reclining. Take a deep breath and notice the bed, couch, or chair. Feel the softness of your blanket. Be thankful that you have the time, money, and inclination to read this book and revel in your journey to achieve your fullest potential!

Did you watch the sunset last night or the sunrise this morning? When was the last time you enjoyed the smell of freshly cut grass? Don't you just love the feel of getting a haircut or having your partner scratch your scalp?

Chapter 12 — Enjoy the Journey

Not a day goes by when I don't think of this quotation I heard years ago by an unknown author. It says:

> Take time to appreciate the little things in life, because the big things may never come, and then you've hung around for nothing.

What do you enjoy?

Right now, create a mental list of the little things that you love and appreciate. Endeavor to take the time to enjoy them and be more mindful.

Remember, find happiness in the *pursuit* of your dreams. Relish and enjoy the journey. Don't hang around for nothing.

This Is It

Have you ever said or thought any of these things?

- Once I am out of debt, then I can relax.
- When I lose weight, I will be happy.
- If I just get this job, then I will have more time for the kids.
- I'll romance my wife more once I am working fewer hours.
- I'll be happy once I get married.
- I'll slow down once my business is up and running.

I used to live in the future and was rarely "mindful in the moment." One day as my dad and I sat on the porch, we talked about how happy and successful I would be once my business got to a new level. Then I could get married and settle down.

Now my dad is no philosopher, God bless him, but what he simply and quietly said rocked my world.

"This is it, Mike."

"What do you mean?" I asked.

"This is it," he repeated.

Again, I asked him to clarify.

"It doesn't get any better than this. Right here. Today. Now. We can't bet on having a tomorrow. It's not going to get any better."

Ever the dreamer, believer, positive thinker, I said, "What do you mean, Dad? Don't you believe that I'm going to make it as a coach? Write a best seller? Become a millionaire? Help lots of people?"

He said, "Maybe. Maybe not. But that's later. For now, this is it. This is life . . . sitting here with your father."

Chapter 12 — Enjoy the Journey

I'd usually want to debate this, but although I had heard similar mantras and platitudes a zillion times, I "got it" in that instant—from my "regular ol' dad."

Are you living today to its fullest?

Be happy now. This is it.

"You Look Awful"

Julie came over to bring lunch and report on the status of the errands she was running. As soon as she opened the door, she said, "What's the matter with *you?* You look awful."

It was noon and I hadn't showered, shaved, or even brushed my teeth! The deadline for my manuscript was fast approaching. It was crunch time. I hadn't slept the night before, hadn't worked out in four days, was eating poorly and drinking little water. My neck was severely kinked up and my laptop crashed before six hours of the previous day's work was saved to a disc. I was grunt personified.

"Just give me my Tums and mind your own business," I shot back at her in jest.

"Oh, so this is how you're *enjoying the journey,*" Julie joked. "Wow, I can't wait to read your book and take your advice!"

Do you think that put me in my place?

From *Grunt* to GREATNESS!

Can you enjoy the process?

It's easy to enjoy the journey when things are going well. It's a challenge—yet so rewarding—to genuinely enjoy the process in the midst of difficulty.

Oh, So Close to Enlightenment

A friend read my manuscript and sent me the following passage from *The Power of Now* by Eckhart Tolle in response to my writing about "being mindful."

> Do you know the story of Banzan? Before he became a great Zen master, he spent many years in the pursuit of enlightenment, but it eluded him. Then one day, as he was walking in the market place, he overheard a conversation between a butcher and his customer. "Give me the best piece of meat you have," said the customer. And the butcher replied, "Every piece of meat I have is the best. There is no piece of meat here that is not the best." Upon hearing this, Banzan became enlightened.

When you accept *what is*—every piece of meat, every moment—as the best, that's enlightenment.

Then jokingly, my friend attached a note saying: "Do you realize how close you are coming to enlightenment?" You already think every good moment is 'the best.' Now all

Chapter 12 — Enjoy the Journey

you have to do is see all the bad ones as the best, too, and you're there!"

How profound. Yes, while most of us think we may be good at finding 'the best' even in moments that are clearly not, I'm sure we all have a long way to go.

Don't you agree?

From *Grunt* to GREATNESS!

13

Celebrate Life

> *"It occurred to him, that what had seemed impossible before . . . that he had not spent his life as he should have, might after all, be true."*
>
> — Leo Tolstoy, *The Death of Ivan Illych*

Written in Stone

It had been 15 years since I returned to Agawam, Massachusetts, my childhood home. The day after Thanksgiving, 2004, was my 20-year high school reunion. My friend Ann and I were on a long morning walk, when we realized we were close to the cemetery where three of my four grandparents are buried. We found the site easily, despite the growth of the cemetery.

As I looked upon the tombstone of my mom's dad, which will be shared by my grandma once she passes, I was drawn to the blank space to be filled in later with her date of death:

From *Grunt* to GREATNESS!

Born		*Died*
1919	Roger H. Newell	1974
1920	Ruth M. Newell	

I was suddenly struck by the "matter of factness" of the blank space—the reality that my grandmother will die and this number will be filled in someday. My grandmother is going to die. I am going to die. You are going to die. As the tombstone indicates and as Ann pointed out the double meaning in her clever way: *It's written in stone.*

Have you considered the certainty of your death?

Imagine your funeral with a few dozen family members and friends reminiscing about your life. What do you want them to be saying? How do you want to be remembered? What do you want to accomplish before you die?

Please, don't simply read these words and think, "I'll have to think about that someday." Think about it now. That's the only time you have—now.

Happy Birthday!

As Og Mandino said in "The God Memorandum" from the book *The Greatest Miracle in the World:*

> This is your birthday. This is your new date of birth . . . Do all things with love . . . love for yourself, love for all others, and love for me . . . Let me cut the grave cloths that have

Chapter 13 — Celebrate Life

bound you. This day you have been notified. You are the greatest miracle in the world.

You *are* the greatest miracle in the world. The very fact that you have desires and dreams is proof that you have within you the capacity to achieve them.

Today is your new birthday, your new date of birth. I challenge you to wake up and stop throwing up over the edge of life. I challenge you to make a conscious decision and take action in pursuit of your personal best in all areas of life. And most of all, I challenge you to love yourself now and truly relish the journey.

I look forward to seeing you on the path *from grunt to greatness*.

From *Grunt* to GREATNESS!

From Grunt to Greatness Services

We are creating a thriving community to support you in your growth from grunt to greatness! Please visit **www.fromgrunttogreatness.com**.

We want to hear from you!

Are you ready to share a success story about your growth from grunt to greatness? We would love to feature you on our website or monthly newsletter.

Join our community...

Please register for our complimentary monthly e-newsletter featuring *FGTG* success stories, complimentary teleclasses, upcoming training sessions, and much more.

Bring the FGTG message to your next event...

Michael is a passionate, funny, charismatic public speaker. The principles in this book can be customized specifically for small business owners, managers, employees, and more. Bring Michael to your association or company for a keynote speech or breakout session. You will be happy you did!

Ready to become a coach yourself?

We are looking for dedicated, passionate people who would like to help others reach their goals and dreams. We will license our material to you and train you to create your own coaching business!

Michael's next book...

FGTG is the first in a series of books. Michael's next book, FGTG: Health & Wellness will be out in winter 2006. Consistent with the humor in this original, H&W promises to be like no other weight loss book you have ever read!

Griffin Merchandise...

If you love Griffin, you'll love our upcoming merchandise line featuring calendars, clothing, coffee mugs, posters, and more. We are dedicated to incorporating Griffin into your life as a constant reminder to love yourself NOW and pursue your personal best!

About Michael

Michael Charest is a personal and business coach, writer and speaker. He is president of *Growth Unlimited,* a company specializing in coaching clients to success using the steps and principles outlined in this book. *Business Growth Solutions,* a division of *Growth Unlimited,* has helped thousands of small business owners grow their businesses and their lives. He is also the founder of *Coach & Grow Rich,* a company he has since sold.

Michael's passion is writing and speaking. He travels internationally delivering high-energy, inspirational, and humorous talks, based on the life experiences and challenges we all share.

Prior to starting his personal development business, Michael was the general manager of a prestigious country club in the LA area.

Originally from Massachusetts, Michael has lived in Redondo Beach, CA for the last few years, but at press time was contemplating his next move. Who knows where he is living as you read this book! For more information on Michael and his company's products and services, please visit **www.fromgrunttogreatness.com.**